THREE PLAYS

SIX CHARACTERS IN SEARCH OF AN AUTHOR—"HENRY IV."—RIGHT YOU ARE! (IF YOU THINK SO)

BY

LUIGI PIRANDELLO

NEW YORK
E. P. DUTTON & COMPANY
681 FIFTH AVENUE

Copyright, 1922,
By E. P. Dutton & Company

All Rights Reserved

This edition is limited to Fifteen Hundred copies.

Performance forbidden and rights of representation reserved. Application for amateur or professional rights of performance of any of these plays must be addressed to the Publishers.

Attention is drawn to the penalties provided by law for any infringement of rights under Section 4966, United States Revised Statutes, Title 60, Chapter 3.

PRINTED IN THE UNITED
STATES OF AMERICA

PREFATORY NOTE

No apology is necessary for offering to American readers a play which critics, with singular unanimity, have called one of the most original productions seen on the modern stage. In less than a year's time, "Six Characters in Search of an Author" has won a distinguished place in the dramatic literature of the Western world, attracting audiences and engaging intellects far removed from the particular influences which made of it a season's sensation in Italy.

Yet the word "original" is not enough, unless we embrace under that characterization qualities far richer than those normally credited to the "trick" play. The "Six Characters" is something more than an unusually ingenious variation of the "play within a play." It is something more than a new twist given to the "dream character" made familiar by the contemporary Italian grotesques. It is a dramatization of the artistic process itself, in relation to the problem of reality and unreality which has engaged Pirandello in one way or another for more than twenty years.

I venture to insist upon this point as against those observers who have tried to see in the "Six Characters" an ironical satire of the commercial drama, as we know it today, mixed, more or less artificially, with a rather obvious philosophy of neo-idealism. No such mixture exists. The blend is organic. The object of Pirandello's bitter irony is not the stage-manager, nor the theatrical producer, nor even the dramatic critic: it is the dramatist; it is the artist; it is, in the end, life itself.

I suppose the human soul presents no mysteries to those

who have been thoroughly grounded in the science of Freud. But in spite of psycho-analysis a few Hamlets still survive. Pirandello is one of them.

What are people really like? In the business of everyday life, nothing is commoner than the categorical judgment sweeping and assured in its affirmatives. But as we cut a little deeply into the living matter of the spirit, the problem becomes more complicated. Do we ever understand the whole motivation of an action—not in others only but even in ourselves?

Oh, yes, there are people who *know*. . . . The State knows, with its laws and its procedures. And society knows, with its conventions. And individuals know, with their formulas for conduct often cannily applied with reference to interest.—The ironical element, as everyone has noted, is fundamental in Pirandello!

Apart from works in his earlier manner (realistic pictures from Southern Italian life, including such gems as "Sicilian Limes"), Pirandello's most distinctive productions have dealt with this general theme. No one of them, indeed, exhausts it. And how could this be otherwise? Pirandello, approaching the sixties, to be sure, is nevertheless in spirit a man of the younger Italian generation, which, trained by Croce and Gentile, has "learned how to think." But however great his delight in playing with "actual idealism," he knows the difference between a drama and a philosophical dissertation. His plays are situations embodying conclusions, simple, or indeed "obvious" in their convincingness. They must be taken as a whole—if one would look for a full statement of Pirandello's "thought."

A "thought," moreover, which may or may not invite us to profound reflection. Enough for the lover of the theatre is the fact that Pirandello derives the most interesting dramatic possibilities from it. Sometimes it is the "reality"

PREFATORY NOTE

which society sees brought into contrast with the reality which action proves (*Il piacere dell'onestà*). Again, it is the "reality" which a man sees in himself thwarted by the reality which actually controls ("*Ma non è una cosa seria*"). In "Right You Are" (*Così è, se vi pare*) we have a general satire of the "cocksure," who, placed in the presence of reality and unreality, are unable to distinguish one from the other.

In the "Six Characters" it is the turn of the artist. Can art—creative art, where the spirit would seem most autonomous—itself determine reality? No, because once "a character is born, he acquires such an independence, even of his own author, that he can be imagined by everybody in situations where the author never dreamed of placing him, and so acquires a meaning which the author never thought of giving him." In this lies the great originality of this very original play—the discovery (so Italian, when one thinks of it, and so novel, as one compares it with the traditional rôle of the "artist" in the European play) that the laborious effort of artistic creation is itself a dramatic theme—so unruly, so assertive, is this thing called "life" ever rising to harass and defeat anyone who would interpret, crystallize, devitalize it.

And beyond the drama lies the poetry, a poetry of mysterious symbolism made up of terror, and rebellion, and pity, and human kindliness. Let us not miss the latter, especially, in the complex mood of all Pirandello's theatre.

* * * *

The three plays of Pirandello, here offered in translations that do not hope to be adequate, are famous specimens of the "new" theatre in Italy. The term "new" is much contested, not only in Italy but abroad. In using the word here it is not necessary to claim that this young, impulsive, fascinatingly boisterous after-the-war Italy is doing things that no one else ever thought of doing. We remain on safe ground if we assert that Pirandello and his associates have broken the bounds set to the old fashioned "sentimental" Latin play.

The motivations of the "old" theatre were largely ethical in character, developing spiritual crises from the conflict of impulses with a rigid framework of law and convention. Dramatic art was, so to speak, a department of geometry, dealing with this or that projection or modification of the triangle. Husbands tearing their hair as wives proved unfaithful; disappointed lovers pining in eternal fidelity to mates beyond their social sphere; cuckolds heroically sheathing the stiletto in deference to a higher law of respectability; widows sending second-hand aspirants to suicide that the sacrament of marriage might remain inviolate:—such were the themes.

And there is no doubt, besides, that this "old" theatre produced works of great beauty and intenseness; since the will in conflict with impulse and triumphing over impulse always presents a subject entrancing in human interest and noble in moral implications.

But the potentialities of drama are more numerous than the permutations of three. The "new" theatre in Italy is "new" in this discovery at least.

* * * *

" 'Henry IV.,' " an equally strong and original variation of the insanity motive, is the first of two plays by Pirandello dealing with a special aspect of the problem of reality and unreality. The second, not yet given to the public, is *Vestire gli ingnudi* (". . . And ye clothed me!"). In the former Pirandello studies a situation where an individual finds a world of unreality thrust upon him, voluntarily reassuming it later on, when tragedy springs from the deeper reality. In "And ye clothed me!" we have a girl who, to fill an empty life of no importance, creates a fiction for herself, only to find it torn violently from her and to be left in a naked reality that is, after all, so unreal.

These two plays indicate the present tendency of Pirandello's rapid production—a tendency that promises even richer results as this interesting author delves more extensively into the mysteries of individual psychology.

"'Henry IV.,'" meanwhile, is before us. It can speak for itself.

* * * *

All of Pirandello's plays are built for acting, and only incidentally for reading. We make this observation with "Right You Are" especially in mind, since that play, above all, is a test for the actor. It is typical of Pirandello for its rapidity, its harshness and its violence—the skill with which the tense tableau is drawn out of pure dialectic, pure "conversation." Moreover, it states a fundamental preoccupation of Pirandello in peculiarly lucid and striking fashion. Perhaps a better rendering of the title *Così è (se vi pare)* will occur to many. Ludwig Lewisohn (happily, I thought) suggested "As You Like It," no less. A possibility, quite in the spirit of Pirandello's title in general, would have been another Shakespearean reminiscence: ". . . and Thinking Makes It So." We have kept something approximating the literal, which would be: "So it is (if you think so)."

The text of the "Six Characters" is that of the translation designated by the author and which was used in the sensational productions of the play given in London and New York.

A. L.

CONTENTS

	PAGE
PREFATORY NOTE	v
SIX CHARACTERS IN SEARCH OF AN AUTHOR — A COMEDY IN THE MAKING	1
"HENRY IV."	73
RIGHT YOU ARE (IF YOU THINK SO!)	149

THREE PLAYS

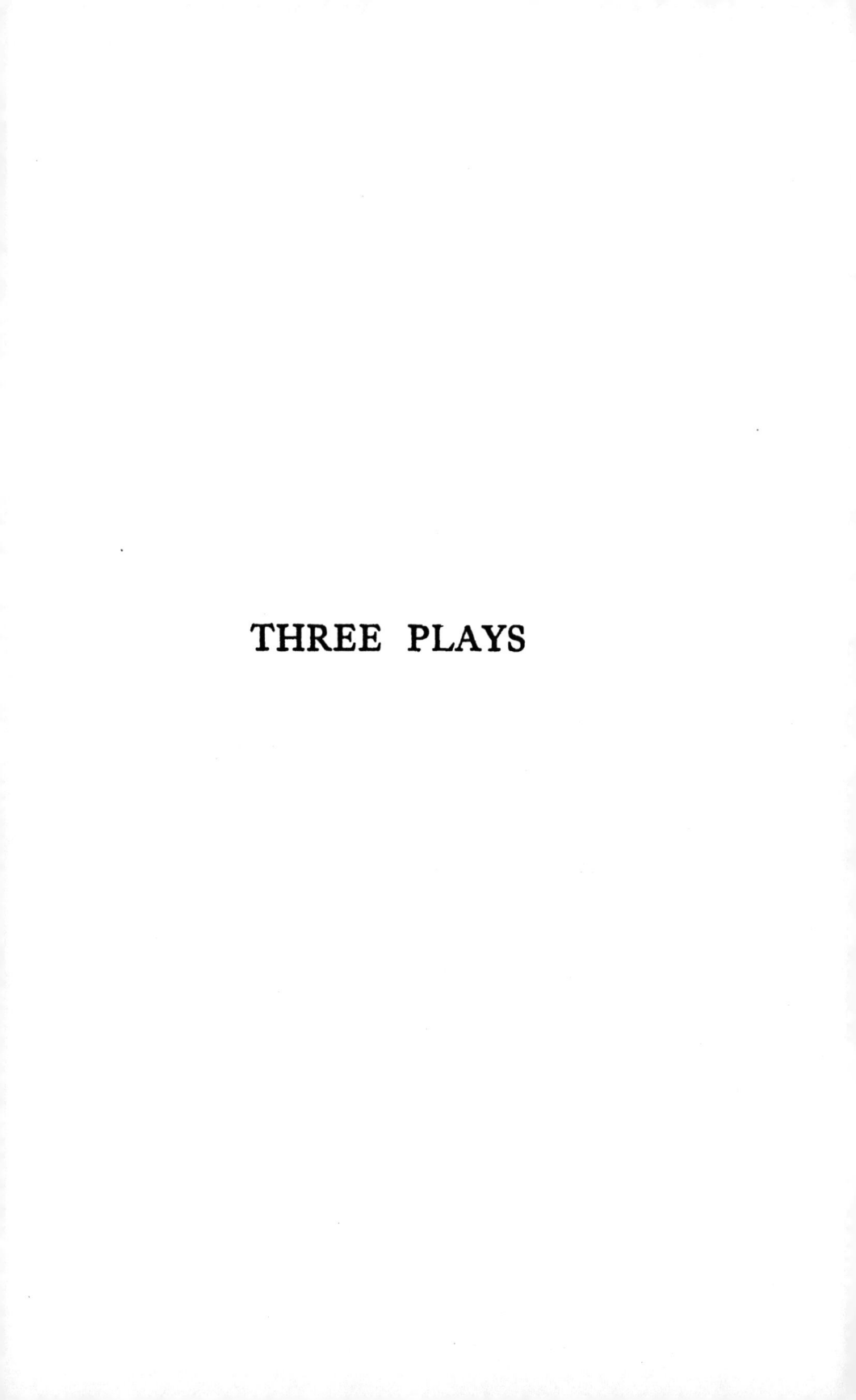

SIX CHARACTERS IN SEARCH OF AN AUTHOR

(Sei personaggi in cerca d'autore)

A COMEDY IN THE MAKING

BY

LUIGI PIRANDELLO

TRANSLATED BY

EDWARD STORER

CHARACTERS OF THE COMEDY IN THE MAKING:

THE FATHER. THE MOTHER. THE STEP-DAUGHTER. THE SON. THE BOY. THE CHILD. (*The last two do not speak.*) MADAME PACE.

ACTORS OF THE COMPANY

THE MANAGER. LEADING LADY. LEADING MAN. SECOND LADY. LEAD. L'INGÉNUE. JUVENILE LEAD. OTHER ACTORS AND ACTRESSES. PROPERTY MAN. PROMPTER. MACHINIST. MANAGER'S SECRETARY. DOOR-KEEPER. SCENE-SHIFTERS.

DAYTIME. THE STAGE OF A THEATRE.

SIX CHARACTERS IN SEARCH OF AN AUTHOR

A COMEDY IN THE MAKING

ACT I.

N. B. The Comedy is without acts or scenes. The performance is interrupted once, without the curtain being lowered, when the manager and the chief characters withdraw to arrange the scenario. A second interruption of the action takes place when, by mistake, the stage hands let the curtain down.

The spectators will find the curtain raised and the stage as it usually is during the day time. It will be half dark, and empty, so that from the beginning the public may have the impression of an impromptu performance.

Prompter's box and a small table and chair for the manager.

Two other small tables and several chairs scattered about as during rehearsals.

The actors and actresses of the company enter from the back of the stage:

first one, then another, then two together: nine or ten in all. They are about to rehearse a Pirandello play: Mixing It Up. *Some of the company move off towards their dressing rooms. The prompter who has the "book" under his arm, is waiting for the manager in order to begin the rehearsal.*

The actors and actresses, some standing, some sitting, chat and smoke. One perhaps reads a paper; another cons his part.

Finally, the Manager enters and goes to the table prepared for him. His secretary brings him his mail, through which he glances. The prompter takes his seat, turns on a light, and opens the "book."

THE MANAGER (*throwing a letter down on the table*). I can't see (*to Property Man*). Let's have a little light, please!

PROPERTY MAN. Yes sir, yes, at once (*a light comes down on to the stage*).

THE MANAGER (*clapping his hands*). Come along! Come along! Second act of "Mixing it Up" (*sits down*).

(*The actors and actresses go from the front of the stage to the wings, all except the three who are to begin the rehearsal*).

THE PROMPTER (*reading the "book"*). "Leo Gala's house. A curious room serving as dining-room and study."

THE MANAGER (*to Property Man*). Fix up the old red room.

PROPERTY MAN (*noting it down*). Red set. All right!

THE PROMPTER (*continuing to read from the "book"*). "Table already laid and writing desk with books and papers. Book-shelves. Exit rear to Leo's bedroom. Exit left to kitchen. Principal exit to right."

THE MANAGER (*energetically*). Well, you understand: The principal exit over there; here, the kitchen. (*Turning to actor who is to play the part of Socrates*). You make your entrances and exits here. (*To Property Man*) The baize doors at the rear, and curtains.

PROPERTY MAN (*noting it down*). Right oh!

PROMPTER (*reading as before*). "When the curtain rises, Leo Gala, dressed in cook's cap and apron is busy beating an egg in a cup. Philip, also dressed as a cook, is beating another egg. Guido Venanzi is seated and listening."

LEADING MAN (*to manager*). Excuse me, but must I absolutely wear a cook's cap?

THE MANAGER (*annoyed*). I imagine so. It says so there anyway (*pointing to the "book"*).

LEADING MAN. But it's ridiculous!

THE MANAGER (*jumping up in a rage*). Ridiculous? Ridiculous? Is it my fault if France won't send us any more good comedies, and we are reduced to putting on Pirandello's works, where nobody understands anything, and where the author plays the fool with us all? (*The actors grin. The Manager goes to Leading Man and shouts*). Yes sir, you put on the cook's cap and beat eggs. Do you suppose that with all this egg-beating business you are on an ordinary stage? Get that out of your head. You represent the shell of the eggs you are beating! (*Laughter and comments among the actors*). Silence! and listen to my explanations, please! (*To Leading Man*): "The empty form of reason without the fullness of instinct, which is blind."—You stand for reason, your wife is instinct. It's a mixing up of the parts, according to which you who act your own part become the puppet of yourself. Do you understand?

LEADING MAN. I'm hanged if I do.

THE MANAGER. Neither do I. But let's get on with it. It's sure to be a glorious failure anyway. (*Confidentially*): But I say, please face three-quarters. Otherwise, what with the abstruseness of the dialogue, and the public that won't be able to hear you, the whole thing will go to hell. Come on! come on!

PROMPTER. Pardon sir, may I get into my box? There's a bit of a draught.

THE MANAGER. Yes, yes, of course!

At this point, the door-keeper has entered from the stage

door and advances towards the manager's table, taking off his braided cap. During this manoeuvre, the Six Characters enter, and stop by the door at back of stage, so that when the door-keeper is about to announce their coming to the Manager, they are already on the stage. A tenuous light surrounds them, almost as if irradiated by them—the faint breath of their fantastic reality.

This light will disappear when they come forward towards the actors. They preserve, however, something of the dream lightness in which they seem almost suspended; but this does not detract from the essential reality of their forms and expressions.

He who is known as THE FATHER is a man of about 50: hair, reddish in colour, thin at the temples; he is not bald, however; thick moustaches, falling over his still fresh mouth, which often opens in an empty and uncertain smile. He is fattish, pale; with an especially wide forehead. He has blue, oval-shaped eyes, very clear and piercing. Wears light trousers and a dark jacket. He is alternatively mellifluous and violent in his manner.

THE MOTHER seems crushed and terrified as if by an intolerable weight of shame and abasement. She is dressed in modest black and wears a thick widow's veil of crêpe. When she lifts this, she reveals a wax-like face. She always keeps her eyes downcast.

THE STEP-DAUGHTER, is dashing, almost impudent, beautiful. She wears mourning too, but with great elegance. She shows contempt for the timid half-frightened manner of the wretched BOY (14 years old, and also dressed in black); on the other hand, she displays a lively tenderness for her little sister, THE CHILD (about four), who is dressed in white, with a black silk sash at the waist.

THE SON (22) tall, severe in his attitude of contempt for

THE FATHER, *supercilious and indifferent to the* MOTHER. *He looks as if he had come on the stage against his will.*

DOOR-KEEPER (*cap in hand*). Excuse me, sir . . .
THE MANAGER (*rudely*). Eh? What is it?
DOOR-KEEPER (*timidly*). These people are asking for you, sir.
THE MANAGER (*furious*). I am rehearsing, and you know perfectly well no one's allowed to come in during rehearsals! (*Turning to the Characters*): Who are you, please? What do you want?
THE FATHER (*coming forward a little, followed by the others who seem embarrassed*). As a matter of fact . . . we have come here in search of an author . . .
THE MANAGER (*half angry, half amazed*). An author? What author?
THE FATHER. Any author, sir.
THE MANAGER. But there's no author here. We are not rehearsing a new piece.
THE STEP-DAUGHTER (*vivaciously*). So much the better, so much the better! We can be your new piece.
AN ACTOR (*coming forward from the others*). Oh, do you hear that?
THE FATHER (*to Step-Daughter*). Yes, but if the author isn't here . . . (*To Manager*) . . . unless you would be willing . . .
THE MANAGER. You are trying to be funny.
THE FATHER. No, for Heaven's sake, what are you saying? We bring you a drama, sir.
THE STEP-DAUGHTER. We may be your fortune.
THE MANAGER. Will you oblige me by going away? We haven't time to waste with mad people.
THE FATHER (*mellifluously*). Oh sir, you know well that life is full of infinite absurdities, which, strangely

enough, do not even need to appear plausible, since they are true.

THE MANAGER. What the devil is he talking about?

THE FATHER. I say that to reverse the ordinary process may well be considered a madness: that is, to create credible situations, in order that they may appear true. But permit me to observe that if this be madness, it is the sole *raison d'être* of your profession, gentlemen. (*The actors look hurt and preplexed*).

THE MANAGER (*getting up and looking at him*). So our profession seems to you one worthy of madmen then?

THE FATHER. Well, to make seem true that which isn't true . . . without any need . . . for a joke as it were . . . Isn't that your mission, gentlemen: to give life to fantastic characters on the stage?

THE MANAGER (*interpreting the rising anger of the Company*). But I would beg you to believe, my dear sir, that the profession of the comedian is a noble one. If today, as things go, the playwrights give us stupid comedies to play and puppets to represent instead of men, remember we are proud to have given life to immortal works here on these very boards! (*The actors, satisfied, applaud their Manager*).

THE FATHER (*interrupting furiously*). Exactly, perfectly, to living beings more alive than those who breathe and wear clothes: beings less real perhaps, but truer! I agree with you entirely. (*The actors look at one another in amazement*).

THE MANAGER. But what do you mean? Before, you said . . .

THE FATHER. No, excuse me, I meant it for you, sir, who were crying out that you had no time to lose with madmen, while no one better than yourself knows that nature uses the instrument of human fantasy in order to pursue her high creative purpose.

THE MANAGER. Very well,—but where does all this take us?

THE FATHER. Nowhere! It is merely to show you that one is born to life in many forms, in many shapes, as tree, or as stone, as water, as butterfly, or as woman. So one may also be born a character in a play.

THE MANAGER (*with feigned comic dismay*). So you and these other friends of yours have been born characters?

THE FATHER. Exactly, and alive as you see! (*Manager and actors burst out laughing*).

THE FATHER (*hurt*). I am sorry you laugh, because we carry in us a drama, as you can guess from this woman here veiled in black.

THE MANAGER (*losing patience at last and almost indignant*). Oh, chuck it! Get away please! Clear out of here! (*to Property Man*). For Heaven's sake, turn them out!

THE FATHER (*resisting*). No, no, look here, we . . .

THE MANAGER (*roaring*). We come here to work, you know.

LEADING ACTOR. One cannot let oneself be made such a fool of.

THE FATHER (*determined, coming forward*). I marvel at your incredulity, gentlemen. Are you not accustomed to see the characters created by an author spring to life in yourselves and face each other? Just because there is no "book" (*pointing to the Prompter's box*) which contains us, you refuse to believe . . .

THE STEP-DAUGHTER (*advances towards Manager, smiling and coquettish*). Believe me, we are really six most interesting characters, sir; side-tracked however.

THE FATHER. Yes, that is the word! (*To Manager all at once*): In the sense, that is, that the author who created us alive no longer wished, or was no longer able, materially to put us into a work of art. And this was a real crime, sir; because he who has had the luck to be born a character can laugh even at death. He cannot die. The man, the writer, the instrument of the creation will die, but his creation does not die. And to live for ever, it does not need to have extraordinary gifts or to be able to work wonders. Who was Sancho Panza? Who was Don Abbondio? Yet they live eternally because—live germs as they were—they had the fortune to find a fecundating matrix, a fantasy which could raise and nourish them: make them live for ever!

THE MANAGER. That is quite all right. But what do you want here, all of you?

THE FATHER. We want to live. .

THE MANAGER (*ironically*). For Eternity?

THE FATHER. No, sir, only for a moment . . . in you.

AN ACTOR. Just listen to him!

LEADING LADY. They want to live, in us . . . !

JUVENILE LEAD (*pointing to the Step-Daughter*). I've no objection, as far as that one is concerned!

THE FATHER. Look here! look here! The comedy has to be made. (*To the Manager*): But if you and your actors are willing, we can soon concert it among ourselves.

THE MANAGER (*annoyed*). But what do you want to concert? We don't go in for concerts here. Here we play dramas and comedies!

THE FATHER. Exactly! That is just why we have come to you.

THE MANAGER. And where is the "book"?

THE FATHER. It is in us! (*The actors laugh*). The drama is in us, and we are the drama. We are impatient to play it. Our inner passion drives us on to this.

THE STEP-DAUGHTER (*disdainful, alluring, treacherous, full of impudence*). My passion, sir! Ah, if you only knew! My passion for him! (*Points to the Father and makes a pretence of embracing him. Then she breaks out into a loud laugh*).

THE FATHER (*angrily*). Behave yourself! And please don't laugh in that fashion.

THE STEP-DAUGHTER. With your permission, gentlemen, I, who am a two months' orphan, will show you how I can dance and sing.

(*Sings and then dances* Prenez garde à Tchou-Thin-Tchou).

> Les chinois sont un peuple malin,
> De Shangaî à Pekin,
> Ils ont mis des écriteux partout:
> Prenez garde à Tchou-Thin-Tchou.

ACTORS and ACTRESSES. Bravo! Well done! Tip-top!

THE MANAGER. Silence! This isn't a café concert, you know! (*Turning to the Father in consternation*): Is she mad?

THE FATHER. Mad? No, she's worse than mad.

THE STEP-DAUGHTER (*to Manager*). Worse? Worse? Listen! Stage this drama for us at once! Then you will see that at a certain moment I . . . when this little darling here . . . (*Takes the Child by the hand and leads her to the Manager*): Isn't she a dear? (*Takes her up and kisses her*). Darling! Darling! (*Puts her down again and adds feelingly*): Well, when God suddenly takes this dear little child away from that poor mother there; and this imbecile here (*seizing hold of the Boy roughly and pushing him forward*) does the stupidest things, like the fool he is, you will see me run away. Yes, gentleman, I shall be off. But the moment hasn't arrived yet. After what has taken place between him and me (*indicates the Father with a horrible wink*), I can't remain any longer in this society, to have to witness the anguish of this mother here for that fool . . . (*indicates the Son*). Look at him! Look at him! See how indifferent, how frigid he is, because he is the legitimate son. He despises me, despises him (*pointing to the Boy*), despises this baby here; because . . . we are bastards (*goes to the Mother and embraces her*). And he doesn't want to recognize her as his mother—she who is the common mother of us all. He looks down upon her as if she were only the mother of us three bastards. Wretch! (*She says all this very rapidly, excitedly. At the word "bastards" she raises her voice, and almost spits out the final "Wretch!"*).

THE MOTHER (*to the Manager, in anguish*). In the name of these two little children, I beg you . . . (*She grows faint and is about to fall*). Oh God!

THE FATHER (*coming forward to support her as do some of the actors*). Quick a chair, a chair for this poor widow!

THE ACTORS. Is it true? Has she really fainted?

THE MANAGER. Quick, a chair! Here!

(*One of the actors brings a chair, the others proffer assistance. The Mother tries to prevent the Father from lifting the veil which covers her face*).

THE FATHER. Look at her! Look at her!

THE MOTHER. No, no; stop it please!

THE FATHER (*raising her veil*). Let them see you!

THE MOTHER (*rising and covering her face with her hands, in desperation*). I beg you, sir, to prevent this man from carrying out his plan which is loathsome to me.

THE MANAGER (*dumbfounded*). I don't understand at all. What is the situation? Is this lady your wife? (*to the Father*).

THE FATHER. Yes, gentlemen: my wife!

THE MANAGER. But how can she be a widow if you are alive? (*The actors find relief for their astonishment in a loud laugh*).

THE FATHER. Don't laugh! Don't laugh like that, for Heaven's sake. Her drama lies just here in this: she has had a lover, a man who ought to be here.

THE MOTHER (*with a cry*). No! No!

THE STEP-DAUGHTER. Fortunately for her, he is dead. Two months ago as I said. We are in mourning, as you see.

THE FATHER. He isn't here you see, not because he is dead. He isn't here—look at her a moment and you will understand—because her drama isn't a drama of the love of two men for whom she was incapable of feeling anything except possibly a little gratitude—gratitude not for me but for the other. She isn't a woman, she is a mother, and her drama—powerful sir, I assure you—lies, as a matter of fact, all in these four children she has had by two men.

THE MOTHER. I had them? Have you got the courage to say that I wanted them? (*To the company*). It was his doing. It was he who gave me that other man, who forced me to go away with him.

THE STEP-DAUGHTER. It isn't true.

THE MOTHER (*startled*). Not true, isn't it?

THE STEP-DAUGHTER. No, it isn't true, it just isn't true.

THE MOTHER. And what can you know about it?

THE STEP-DAUGHTER. It isn't true. Don't believe it. (*To Manager*). Do you know why she says so? For that fellow there (*indicates the Son*). She tortures herself, destroys herself on account of the neglect of that son there; and she wants him to believe that if she abandoned him when he was only two years old, it was because he (*indicates the Father*) made her do so.

THE MOTHER (*vigorously*). He forced me to it, and I call God to witness it (*to the Manager*). Ask him (*in-*

dicates husband) if it isn't true. Let him speak. You (*to daughter*) are not in a position to know anything about it.

THE STEP-DAUGHTER. I know you lived in peace and happiness with my father while he lived. Can you deny it?

THE MOTHER. No, I don't deny it . . .

THE STEP-DAUGHTER. He was always full of affection and kindness for you (*to the Boy, angrily*). It's true, isn't it? Tell them! Why don't you speak, you little fool?

THE MOTHER. Leave the poor boy alone. Why do you want to make me appear ungrateful, daughter? I don't want to offend your father. I have answered him that I didn't abandon my house and my son through any fault of mine, nor from any wilful passion.

THE FATHER. It is true. It was my doing.

LEADING MAN (*to the Company*). What a spectacle!

LEADING LADY. We are the audience this time.

JUVENILE LEAD. For once, in a way.

THE MANAGER (*beginning to get really interested*). Let's hear them out. Listen!

THE SON. Oh yes, you're going to hear a fine bit now. He will talk to you of the Demon of Experiment.

THE FATHER. You are a cynical imbecile. I've told you so already a hundred times (*to the Manager*). He tries to make fun of me on account of this expression which I have found to excuse myself with.

THE SON (*with disgust*). Yes, phrases! phrases!

THE FATHER. Phrases! Isn't everyone consoled when faced with a trouble or fact he doesn't understand, by a word, some simple word, which tells us nothing and yet calms us?

THE STEP-DAUGHTER. Even in the case of remorse. In fact, especially then.

THE FATHER. Remorse? No, that isn't true. I've done more than use words to quieten the remorse in me.

THE STEP-DAUGHTER. Yes, there was a bit of money too. Yes, yes, a bit of money. There were the hundred lire he was about to offer me in payment, gentlemen . . . (*sensation of horror among the actors*).

THE SON (*to the Step-Daughter*). This is vile.

THE STEP-DAUGHTER. Vile? There they were in a pale blue envelope on a little mahogany table in the back of Madame Pace's shop. You know Madame Pace—one of those ladies who attract poor girls of good family into their ateliers, under the pretext of their selling *robes et manteaux*.

THE SON. And he thinks he has bought the right to tyrannise over us all with those hundred lire he was going to pay; but which, fortunately—note this, gentlemen—he had no chance of paying.

THE STEP-DAUGHTER. It was a near thing, though, you know! (*laughs ironically*).

THE MOTHER (*protesting.*) Shame, my daughter, shame!

THE STEP-DAUGHTER. Shame indeed! This is my revenge! I am dying to live that scene . . . The room . . . I see it . . . Here is the window with the mantles exposed, there the divan, the looking-glass, a screen, there in front of the window the little mahogany table with the blue envelope containing one hundred lire. I see it. I see it. I could take hold of it . . . But you, gentlemen, you ought to turn your backs now: I am almost nude, you know. But I don't blush: I leave that to him (*indicating Father*).

THE MANAGER. I don't understand this at all.

THE FATHER. Naturally enough. I would ask you, sir, to exercise your authority a little here, and let me speak before you believe all she is trying to blame me with. Let me explain.

THE STEP-DAUGHTER. Ah yes, explain it in your own way.

THE FATHER. But don't you see that the whole trouble

lies here. In words, words. Each one of us has within him a whole world of things, each man of us his own special world. And how can we ever come to an understanding if I put in the words I utter the sense and value of things as I see them; while you who listen to me must inevitably translate them according to the conception of things each one of you has within himself. We think we understand each other, but we never really do. Look here! This woman (*indicating the Mother*) takes all my pity for her as a specially ferocious form of cruelty.

THE MOTHER. But you drove me away.

THE FATHER. Do you hear her? I drove her away! She believes I really sent her away.

THE MOTHER. You know how to talk, and I don't; but, believe me sir, (*to Manager*) after he had married me . . . who knows why? . . . I was a poor insignificant woman . . .

THE FATHER. But, good Heavens! it was just for your humility that I married you. I loved this simplicity in you (*He stops when he sees she makes signs to contradict him, opens his arms wide in sign of desperation, seeing how hopeless it is to make himself understood*). You see she denies it. Her mental deafness, believe me, is phenomenal, the limit (*touches his forehead*): deaf, deaf, mentally deaf! She has plenty of feeling. Oh yes, a good heart for the children; but the brain — deaf, to the point of desperation——!

THE STEP-DAUGHTER. Yes, but ask him how his intelligence has helped us.

THE FATHER. If we could see all the evil that may spring from good, what should we do? (*At this point the Leading Lady who is biting her lips with rage at seeing the Leading Man flirting with the Step-Daughter, comes forward and says to the Manager*).

LEADING LADY. Excuse me, but are we going to rehearse today?

MANAGER. Of course, of course; but let's hear them out.

JUVENILE LEAD. This is something quite new.

L'INGÉNUE. Most interesting!

LEADING LADY. Yes, for the people who like that kind of thing (*casts a glance at Leading Man*).

THE MANAGER (*to Father.*) You must please explain yourself quite clearly (*sits down*).

THE FATHER. Very well then: listen! I had in my service a poor man, a clerk, a secretary of mine, full of devotion, who became friends with her (*indicating the Mother*). They understood one another, were kindred souls in fact, without, however, the least suspicion of any evil existing. They were incapable even of thinking of it.

THE STEP-DAUGHTER. So he thought of it—for them!

THE FATHER. That's not true. I meant to do good to them—and to myself, I confess, at the same time. Things had come to the point that I could not say a word to either of them without their making a mute appeal, one to the other, with their eyes. I could see them silently asking each other how I was to be kept in countenance, how I was to be kept quiet. And this, believe me, was just about enough of itself to keep me in a constant rage, to exasperate me beyond measure.

THE MANAGER. And why didn't you send him away then—this secretary of yours?

THE FATHER. Precisely what I did, sir. And then I had to watch this poor woman drifting forlornly about the house like an animal without a master, like an animal one has taken in out of pity.

THE MOTHER. Ah yes . . . !

THE FATHER (*suddenly turning to the Mother*). It's true about the son anyway, isn't it?

THE MOTHER. He took my son away from me first of all.

THE FATHER. But not from cruelty. I did it so that he should grow up healthy and strong by living in the country.

THE STEP-DAUGHTER (*pointing to him ironically*). As one can see.

THE FATHER (*quickly*). Is it my fault if he has grown up like this? I sent him to a wet nurse in the country, a peasant, as *she* did not seem to me strong enough, though she is of humble origin. That was, anyway, the reason I married her. Unpleasant all this maybe, but how can it be helped? My mistake possibly, but there we are! All my life I have had these confounded aspirations towards a certain moral sanity. (*At this point the Step-Daughter bursts out into a noisy laugh*). Oh, stop, it! Stop it! I can't stand it.

THE MANAGER. Yes, please stop it, for Heaven's sake.

THE STEP-DAUGHTER. But imagine moral sanity from him, if you please—the client of certain ateliers like that of Madame Pace!

THE FATHER. Fool! That is the proof that I am a man! This seeming contradiction, gentlemen, is the strongest proof that I stand here a live man before you. Why, it is just for this very incongruity in my nature that I have had to suffer what I have. I could not live by the side of that woman (*indicating the Mother*) any longer; but not so much for the boredom she inspired me with as for the pity I felt for her.

THE MOTHER. And so he turned me out—.

THE FATHER. —well provided for! Yes, I sent her to that man, gentlemen . . . to let her go free of me.

THE MOTHER. And to free himself.

THE FATHER. Yes, I admit it. It was also a liberation for me. But great evil has come of it. I meant well when I did it; and I did it more for her sake than mine. I swear it (*crosses his arms on his chest; then turns suddenly to the Mother*). Did I ever lose sight of you until that other man carried you off to another town, like the angry fool he was? And on account of my pure interest in you . . . my pure interest, I repeat, that had no base motive in it . . . I watched with the tenderest concern the new family that grew up around her. She can bear witness to this (*points to the Step-Daughter*).

THE STEP-DAUGHTER. Oh yes, that's true enough. When I was a kiddie, so so high, you know, with plaits over my shoulders and knickers longer than my skirts, I used to see him waiting outside the school for me to come out. He came to see how I was growing up.

THE FATHER. This is infamous, shameful!

THE STEP-DAUGHTER. No, Why?

THE FATHER. Infamous! infamous! (*Then excitedly to Manager explaining*). After she (*indicating Mother*) went away, my house seemed suddenly empty. She was my incubus, but she filled my house. I was like a dazed fly alone in the empty rooms. This boy here (*indicating the Son*) was educated away from home, and when he came back, he seemed to me to be no more mine. With no mother to stand between him and me, he grew up entirely for himself, on his own, apart, with no tie of intellect or affection binding him to me. And then—strange but true—I was driven, by curiosity at first and then by some tender sentiment, towards her family, which had come into being through my will. The thought of her began gradually to fill up the emptiness I felt all around me. I wanted to know if she were happy in living out the simple daily duties of life. I wanted to think of her as fortunate and happy because far away from the complicated torments of my spirit. And so, to have proof of this, I used to watch that child coming out of school.

THE STEP-DAUGHTER. Yes, yes. True. He used to follow me in the street and smiled at me, waved his hand, like this. I would look at him with interest, wondering who he might be. I told my mother, who guessed at once (*the Mother agrees with a nod*). Then she didn't want to send me to school for some days; and when I finally went back, there he was again—looking so ridiculous—with a paper parcel in his hands. He came close to me, caressed me, and drew out a fine straw hat from the parcel, with a bouquet of flowers—all for me!

THE MANAGER. A bit discursive this, you know!

THE SON (*contemptuously*). Literature! Literature!

THE FATHER. Literature indeed! This is life, this is passion!

THE MANAGER. It may be, but it won't act.

THE FATHER. I agree. This is only the part leading up. I don't suggest this should be staged. She (*pointing to the Step-Daughter*), as you see, is no longer the flapper with plaits down her back—.

THE STEP-DAUGHTER. —and the knickers showing below the skirt!

THE FATHER. The drama is coming now, sir; something new, complex, most interesting.

THE STEP-DAUGHTER. As soon as my father died . . .

THE FATHER. —there was absolute misery for them. They came back here, unknown to me. Through her stupidity (*pointing to the Mother*)! It is true she can barely write her own name; but she could anyhow have got her daughter to write to me that they were in need . . .

THE MOTHER. And how was I to divine all this sentiment in him?

THE FATHER. That is exactly your mistake, never to have guessed any of my sentiments.

THE MOTHER. After so many years apart, and all that had happened . . .

THE FATHER. Was it my fault if that fellow carried you away? It happened quite suddenly; for after he had obtained some job or other, I could find no trace of them; and so, not unnaturally, my interest in them dwindled. But the drama culminated unforeseen and violent on their return, when I was impelled by my miserable flesh that still lives . . . Ah! what misery, what wretchedness is that of the man who is alone and disdains debasing *liaisons!* Not old enough to do without women, and not young enough to go and look for one without shame. Misery? It's worse than misery; it's a horror; for no woman can any longer give him love; and when a man feels this . . . One ought to do without, you say? Yes, yes, I know. Each of us when he appears before his fellows is clothed in a certain dignity. But every man knows what unconfessable things pass within the secrecy of his own heart. One gives way to the temptation, only to rise from it again, afterwards, with a great eagerness to reestablish one's dignity, as if it were a tombstone to place on the grave of one's shame, and a monument to hide and sign the memory of our weaknesses. Everybody's in the same case. Some folks haven't the courage to say certain things, that's all!

THE STEP-DAUGHTER. All appear to have the courage to do them though.

THE FATHER. Yes, but in secret. Therefore, you want more courage to say these things. Let a man but speak these things out, and folks at once label him a cynic. But it isn't true. He is like all the others, better indeed, because he isn't afraid to reveal with the light of the intelligence the red shame of human bestiality on which most men close their eyes so as not to see it.

Woman—for example, look at her case! She turns tantalizing inviting glances on you. You seize her. No sooner does she feel herself in your grasp than she closes her eyes. It is the sign of her mission, the sign by which she says to man: "Blind yourself, for I am blind."

THE STEP-DAUGHTER. Sometimes she can close them no more: when she no longer feels the need of hiding her shame to herself, but dry-eyed and dispassionately, sees only that of the man who has blinded himself without love. Oh, all these intellectual complications make me sick, disgust me—all this philosophy that uncovers the beast in man, and then seeks to save him, excuse him . . . I can't stand it, sir. When a man seeks to "simplify" life bestially, throwing aside every relic of humanity, every chaste aspiration, every pure feeling, all sense of ideality, duty, modesty, shame . . . then nothing is more revolting and nauseous than a certain kind of remorse—crocodiles' tears, that's what it is.

THE MANAGER. Let's come to the point. This is only discussion.

THE FATHER. Very good, sir! But a fact is like a sack which won't stand up when it is empty. In order that it may stand up, one has to put into it the reason and sentiment which have caused it to exist. I couldn't possibly know that after the death of that man, they had decided to return here, that they were in misery, and that she (*pointing to the Mother*) had gone to work as a modiste, and at a shop of the type of that of Madame Pace.

THE STEP-DAUGHTER. A real high-class modiste, you must know, gentlemen. In appearance, she works for the leaders of the best society; but she arranges matters so that these elegant ladies serve her purpose . . . without prejudice to other ladies who are . . . well . . . only so so.

THE MOTHER. You will believe me, gentlemen, that it never entered my mind that the old hag offered me work because she had her eye on my daughter.

THE STEP-DAUGHTER. Poor mamma! Do you know, sir, what that woman did when I brought her back the work my mother had finished? She would point out to me that I had torn one of my frocks, and she would give it back to my mother to mend. It was I who paid for it, always I; while this poor creature here believed she was sacrificing herself for me and these two children here, sitting up at night sewing Madame Pace's robes.

THE MANAGER. And one day you met there . . .

THE STEP-DAUGHTER. Him, him. Yes sir, an old client. There's a scene for you to play! Superb!

THE FATHER. She, the Mother arrived just then . . .

THE STEP-DAUGHTER (*treacherously*). Almost in time!

THE FATHER (*crying out*). No, in time! in time! Fortunately I recognized her . . . in time. And I took them back home with me to my house. You can imagine now her position and mine: she, as you see her; and I who cannot look her in the face.

THE STEP-DAUGHTER. Absurd! How can I possibly be expected—after that—to be a modest young miss, a fit person to go with his confounded aspirations for "a solid moral sanity"?

THE FATHER. For the drama lies all in this—in the conscience that I have, that each one of us has. We believe this conscience to be a single thing, but it is many-sided. There is one for this person, and another for that. Diverse consciences. So we have this illusion of being one person for all, of having a personality that is unique in all our acts. But it isn't true. We perceive this when, tragically perhaps, in something we do, we are as it were, suspended, caught up in the air on a kind of hook. Then we perceive that all of us was not in that act, and that it would be an atrocious injustice to judge us by that action alone, as if all our existence were summed up in that one deed. Now do you understand the perfidy of this girl? She surprised me in a place, where she ought not to have known me, just as I could not exist for her; and she now seeks to attach to me a reality such as I could never suppose I should have to assume for her in a shameful and fleeting moment of my life. I feel this above all else. And the drama, you will see, acquires a tremendous value from this point. Then there is the position of the others . . . his . . . (*indicating the Son*).

THE SON (*shrugging his shoulders scornfully*). Leave me alone! I don't come into this.

THE FATHER. What? You don't come into this?

THE SON. I've got nothing to do with it, and don't want to have; because you know well enough I wasn't made to be mixed up in all this with the rest of you.

THE STEP-DAUGHTER. We are only vulgar folk! He is the fine gentleman. You may have noticed, Mr. Manager, that I fix him now and again with a look of scorn while he lowers his eyes—for he knows the evil he has done me.

THE SON (*scarcely looking at her*). I?

THE STEP-DAUGHTER. You! you! I owe my life on the streets to you. Did you or did you not deny us, with your behaviour, I won't say the intimacy of home, but even that mere hospitality which makes guests feel at their ease? We were intruders who had come to disturb the kingdom of your legitimacy. I should like to have you witness, Mr. Manager, certain scenes between him and me. He says I have tyrannized over everyone. But it was just his behaviour which made me insist on the reason for which I had come into the house,—this reason he calls "vile"—into his house, with my mother who is his mother too. And I came as mistress of the house.

THE SON. It's easy for them to put me always in the wrong. But imagine, gentlemen, the position of a son, whose fate it is to see arrive one day at his home a young woman of impudent bearing, a young woman who inquires for his father, with whom who knows what business she has. This young man has then to witness her return bolder than ever, accompanied by that child there. He is obliged to watch her treat his father in an equivocal and confidential manner. She asks money of him in a way that lets one suppose he must give it her, *must,* do you understand, because he has every obligation to do so.

THE FATHER. But I have, as a matter of fact, this obligation. I owe it to your mother.

THE SON. How should I know? When had I ever seen or heard of her? One day there arrive with her (*indicating Step-Daughter*) that lad and this baby here. I am told: "This is *your* mother too, you know." I divine from her manner (*indicating Step-Daughter again*) why it is they have come home. I had rather not say what I feel and think about it. I shouldn't even care to confess to myself. No action can therefore be hoped for from me in this affair. Believe me, Mr. Manager, I am an "unrealized" character, dramatically speaking; and I find myself not at all at ease in their company. Leave me out of it, I beg you.

THE FATHER. What? It is just because you are so that . . .

THE SON. How do you know what I am like? When did you ever bother your head about me?

THE FATHER. I admit it. I admit it. But isn't that a situation in itself? This aloofness of yours which is so cruel to me and to your mother, who returns home and sees you almost for the first time grown up, who doesn't recognize you but knows you are her son . . . (*pointing out the Mother to the Manager*). See, she's crying!

THE STEP-DAUGHTER (*angrily, stamping her foot*). Like a fool!

THE FATHER (*indicating Step-Daughter*). She can't

stand him you know. (*Then referring again to the Son*): He says he doesn't come into the affair, whereas he is really the hinge of the whole action. Look at that lad who is always clinging to his mother, frightened and humiliated. It is on account of this fellow here. Possibly his situation is the most painful of all. He feels himself a stranger more than the others. The poor little chap feels mortified, humiliated at being brought into a home out of charity as it were. (*In confidence*)—: He is the image of his father. Hardly talks at all. Humble and quiet.

THE MANAGER. Oh, we'll cut him out. You've no notion what a nuisance boys are on the stage . . .

THE FATHER. He disappears soon, you know. And the baby too. She is the first to vanish from the scene. The drama consists finally in this: when that mother re-enters my house, her family born outside of it, and shall we say superimposed on the original, ends with the death of the little girl, the tragedy of the boy and the flight of the elder daughter. It cannot go on, because it is foreign to its surroundings. So after much torment, we three remain: I, the mother, that son. Then, owing to the disappearance of that extraneous family, we too find ourselves strange to one another. We find we are living in an atmosphere of mortal desolation which is the revenge, as he (*indicating Son*) scornfully said of the Demon of Experiment, that unfortunately hides in me. Thus, sir, you see when faith is lacking, it becomes impossible to create certain states of happiness, for we lack the necessary humility. Vaingloriously, we try to substitute ourselves for this faith, creating thus for the rest of the world a reality which we believe after their fashion, while, actually, it doesn't exist. For each one of us has his own reality to be respected before God, even when it is harmful to one's very self.

THE MANAGER. There is something in what you say.

I assure you all this interests me very much. I begin to think there's the stuff for a drama in all this, and not a bad drama either.

THE STEP-DAUGHTER (*coming forward*). When you've got a character like me.

THE FATHER (*shutting her up, all excited to learn the decision of the Manager*). You be quiet!

THE MANAGER (*reflecting, heedless of interruption*). It's new . . . hem . . . yes . . .

THE FATHER. Absolutely new!

THE MANAGER. You've got a nerve though, I must say, to come here and fling it at me like this . . .

THE FATHER. You will understand, sir, born as we are for the stage . . .

THE MANAGER. Are you amateur actors then?

THE FATHER. No. I say born for the stage, because . . .

THE MANAGER. Oh, nonsense. You're an old hand, you know.

THE FATHER. No sir, no. We act that rôle for which we have been cast, that rôle which we are given in life. And in my own case, passion itself, as usually happens, becomes a trifle theatrical when it is exalted.

THE MANAGER. Well, well, that will do. But you see, without an author . . . I could give you the address of an author if you like . . .

THE FATHER. No, no. Look here! You must be the author.

THE MANAGER. I? What are you talking about?

THE FATHER. Yes, you, you! Why not?

THE MANAGER. Because I have never been an author: that's why.

THE FATHER. Then why not turn author now? Everybody does it. You don't want any special qualities. Your task is made much easier by the fact that we are all here alive before you . . .

THE MANAGER. It won't do.

THE FATHER. What? When you see us live our drama . . .

THE MANAGER. Yes, that's all right. But you want someone to write it.

THE FATHER. No, no. Someone to take it down, possibly, while we play it, scene by scene! It will be enough to sketch it out at first, and then try it over.

THE MANAGER. Well . . . I am almost tempted. It's a bit of an idea. One might have a shot at it.

THE FATHER. Of course. You'll see what scenes will come out of it. I can give you one, at once . . .

THE MANAGER. By Jove, it tempts me. I'd like to have a go at it. Let's try it out. Come with me to my office (*turning to the Actors*). You are at liberty for a bit, but don't stop out of the theatre for long. In a quarter of an hour, twenty minutes, all back here again! (*To the Father*): We'll see what can be done. Who knows if we don't get something really extraordinary out of it?

THE FATHER. There's no doubt about it. They (*indicating the Characters*) had better come with us too, hadn't they?

THE MANAGER. Yes, yes. Come on! come on! (*Moves away and then turning to the actors*): Be punctual, please! (*Manager and the Six Characters cross the stage and go off. The other actors remain, looking at one another in astonishment*).

LEADING MAN. Is he serious? What the devil does he want to do?

JUVENILE LEAD. This is rank madness.

THIRD ACTOR. Does he expect to knock up a drama in five minutes?

JUVENILE LEAD. Like the improvisers!

LEADING LADY. If he thinks I'm going to take part in a joke like this . . .

JUVENILE LEAD. I'm out of it anyway.

FOURTH ACTOR. I should like to know who they are (*alludes to Characters*).

THIRD ACTOR. What do you suppose? Madmen or rascals!

JUVENILE LEAD. And he takes them seriously!

L'INGÉNUE. Vanity! He fancies himself as an author now.

LEADING MAN. It's absolutely unheard of. If the stage has come to this . . . well I'm . . .

FIFTH ACTOR. It's rather a joke.

THIRD ACTOR. Well, we'll see what's going to happen next.

(*Thus talking, the actors leave the stage; some going out by the little door at the back; others retiring to their dressing-rooms.*

The curtain remains up.

The action of the play is suspended for twenty minutes).

ACT II.

The stage call-bells ring to warn the company that the play is about to begin again.

THE STEP-DAUGHTER *comes out of the Manager's office along with* THE CHILD *and* THE BOY. *As she comes out of the office, she cries:—*

Nonsense! nonsense! Do it yourselves! I'm not going to mix myself up in this mess. (*Turning to the Child and coming quickly with her on to the stage*): Come on, Rosetta, let's run!

(THE BOY *follows them slowly, remaining a little behind and seeming perplexed*).

THE STEP-DAUGHTER. (*Stops, bends over the Child and takes the latter's face between her hands*). My little darling! You're frightened, aren't you? You don't know where we are, do you? (*Pretending to reply to a question of the Child*): What is the stage? It's a place, baby, you know, where people play at being serious, a place where they act comedies. We've got to act a comedy now, dead serious, you know; and you're in it also, little one. (*Embraces her, pressing the little head to her breast, and rocking the child for a moment*). Oh darling, darling, what a horrid comedy you've got to play! What a wretched part they've found for you! A garden . . . a fountain . . . look . . . just suppose, kiddie, it's here. Where, you say? Why, right here in the middle. It's all pretence you know. That's the trouble, my pet: it's all make-believe here. It's better to imagine it though, because if they fix it up for you, it'll only be painted cardboard, painted cardboard for the rockery, the water, the plants . . . Ah, but I think a baby like this one would sooner have a make-believe fountain than a real one, so she could play with it. What a joke it'll be for the others! But for you, alas! not quite such a joke: you who are real, baby dear, and really play by a real fountain that is big and green and beautiful, with ever so many bamboos around it that are reflected in the water, and a whole lot of little ducks swimming about . . . No, Rosetta, no, your mother doesn't bother about you on account of that wretch of a son there. I'm in the devil of a temper, and as for that lad . . . (*Seizes Boy by the arm to force him to take one of his hands out of his pockets*). What have you got there? What are you hiding? (*Pulls his hand out of his pocket, looks into it and catches the glint of a revolver*). Ah! where did you get this?

(THE BOY, *very pale in the face, looks at her, but does not answer*).

Idiot! If I'd been in your place, instead of killing myself, I'd have shot one of those two, or both of them: father and son.

(THE FATHER *enters from the office, all excited from his work.* THE MANAGER *follows him*).

THE FATHER. Come on, come on dear! Come here for a minute! We've arranged everything. It's all fixed up.

THE MANAGER (*also excited*). If you please, young lady, there are one or two points to settle still. Will you come along?

THE STEP-DAUGHTER (*following him towards the office*). Ouff! what's the good, if you've arranged everything.

(THE FATHER, MANAGER *and* STEP-DAUGHTER *go back into the office again* (*off*) *for a moment. At the same time,* THE SON *followed by* THE MOTHER, *comes out*).

THE SON (*looking at the three entering office*). Oh this is fine, fine! And to think I can't even get away!

(THE MOTHER *attempts to look at him, but lowers her eyes immediately when he turns away from her. She then sits down.* THE BOY *and* THE CHILD *approach her. She casts a glance again at the Son, and speaks with humble tones, trying to draw him into conversation*).

THE MOTHER. And isn't my punishment the worst of all? (*Then seeing from the Son's manner that he will not bother himself about her*). My God! Why are you so cruel? Isn't it enough for one person to support all this torment? Must you then insist on others seeing it also?

THE SON (*half to himself, meaning the Mother to hear, however*). And they want to put it on the stage! If there was at least a reason for it! He thinks he has got at the meaning of it all. Just as if each one of us in every circumstance of life couldn't find his own explanation of it! (*Pauses*). He complains he was discovered in a place where he ought not to have been seen, in a moment of his life which ought to have remained hidden and kept out of the reach of that convention which he has to maintain for other people. And what about my case? Haven't I had to reveal what no son ought ever to reveal: how father and mother live and are man and wife for themselves quite apart from that idea of father and mother which we give them? When this idea is revealed, our life is then linked at one point only to that man and that woman; and as such it should shame them, shouldn't it?

THE MOTHER *hides her face in her hands. From the dressing-rooms and the little door at the back of the stage the actors and* STAGE MANAGER *return, followed by the* PROPERTY MAN, *and the* PROMPTER. *At the same moment,* THE MANAGER *comes out of his office, accompanied by the* FATHER *and the* STEP-DAUGHTER.

THE MANAGER. Come on, come on, ladies and gentlemen! Heh! you there, machinist!

MACHINIST. Yes sir?

THE MANAGER. Fix up the white parlor with the floral decorations. Two wings and a drop with a door will do. Hurry up!

(THE MACHINIST *runs off at once to prepare the scene, and arranges it while* THE MANAGER *talks with the* STAGE MANAGER, *the* PROPERTY MAN, *and the* PROMPTER *on matters of detail*).

THE MANAGER (*to Property Man*). Just have a look, and see if there isn't a sofa or divan in the wardrobe . . .

PROPERTY MAN. There's the green one.

THE STEP-DAUGHTER. No no! Green won't do. It was yellow, ornamented with flowers—very large! and most comfortable!

PROPERTY MAN. There isn't one like that.

THE MANAGER. It doesn't matter. Use the one we've got.

THE STEP-DAUGHTER. Doesn't matter? It's most important!

THE MANAGER. We're only trying it now. Please don't interfere. (*To Property Man*): See if we've got a shop window—long and narrowish.

THE STEP-DAUGHTER. And the little table! The little mahogany table for the pale blue envelope!

PROPERTY MAN (*To Manager*). There's that little gilt one.

THE MANAGER. That'll do fine.

THE FATHER. A mirror.

THE STEP-DAUGHTER. And the screen! We must have a screen. Otherwise how can I manage?

PROPERTY MAN. That's all right, Miss. We've got any amount of them.

THE MANAGER (*to the Step-Daughter*). We want some clothes pegs too, don't we?

THE STEP-DAUGHTER. Yes, several, several!

THE MANAGER. See how many we've got and bring them all.

PROPERTY MAN. All right!

(THE PROPERTY MAN *hurries off to obey his orders. While he is putting the things in their places, the* MANAGER *talks to the* PROMPTER *and then with the Characters and the actors*).

THE MANAGER (*to Prompter*). Take your seat. Look here: this is the outline of the scenes, act by act (*hands him some sheets of paper*). And now I'm going to ask you to do something out of the ordinary.

PROMPTER. Take it down in shorthand?

THE MANAGER (*pleasantly surprised*). Exactly! Can you do shorthand?

PROMPTER. Yes, a little.

MANAGER. Good! (*Turning to a stage hand*): Go and get some paper from my office, plenty, as much as you can find.

(*The stage hand goes off, and soon returns with a handful of paper which he gives to the Prompter*).

THE MANAGER (*To Prompter*). You follow the scenes as we play them, and try and get the points down, at any rate the most important ones. (*Then addressing the actors*): Clear the stage, ladies and gentlemen! Come over here (*pointing to the Left*) and listen attentively.

LEADING LADY. But, excuse me, we . . .

THE MANAGER (*guessing her thought*). Don't worry! You won't have to improvise.

LEADING MAN. What have we to do then?

THE MANAGER. Nothing. For the moment you just watch and listen. Everybody will get his part written out afterwards. At present we're going to try the thing as best we can. They're going to act now.

THE FATHER (*as if fallen from the clouds into the confusion of the stage*). We? What do you mean, if you please, by a rehearsal?

THE MANAGER. A rehearsal for them (*points to the actors*).

THE FATHER. But since we are the characters . . .

THE MANAGER. All right: "characters" then, if you insist on calling yourselves such. But here, my dear sir, the characters don't act. Here the actors do the acting. The characters are there, in the "book" (*pointing towards Prompter's box*)—when there is a "book"!

THE FATHER. I won't contradict you; but excuse me, the actors aren't the characters. They want to be, they pretend to be, don't they? Now if these gentlemen here are fortunate enough to have us alive before them . . .

THE MANAGER. Oh this is grand! You want to come before the public yourselves then?

THE FATHER. As we are . . .

THE MANAGER. I can assure you it would be a magnificent spectacle!

LEADING MAN. What's the use of us here anyway then?

THE MANAGER. You're not going to pretend that you can act? It makes me laugh! (*The actors laugh*). There, you see, they are laughing at the notion. But, by the way, I must cast the parts. That won't be difficult. They cast themselves. (*To the Second Lady Lead*): You play the Mother. (*To the Father*): We must find her a name.

THE FATHER. Amalia, sir.

THE MANAGER. But that is the real name of your wife. We don't want to call her by her real name.

THE FATHER. Why ever not, if it is her name? . . .

Still, perhaps, if that lady must . . . (*makes a slight motion of the hand to indicate the Second Lady Lead*). I see this woman here (*means the Mother*) as Amalia. But do as you like (*gets more and more confused*). I don't know what to say to you. Already, I begin to hear my own words ring false, as if they had another sound . . .

THE MANAGER. Don't you worry about it. It'll be our job to find the right tones. And as for her name, if you want her Amalia, Amalia it shall be; and if you don't like it, we'll find another! For the moment though, we'll call the characters in this way: (*to* Juvenile Lead) You are the Son; (*to the Leading Lady*) You naturally are the Step-Daughter . . .

THE STEP-DAUGHTER (excitedly). What? what? I, that woman there? (*Bursts out laughing*).

THE MANAGER (*angry*). What is there to laugh at?

LEADING LADY (*indignant*). Nobody has ever dared to laugh at me. I insist on being treated with respect; otherwise I go away.

THE STEP-DAUGHTER. No, no, excuse me . . . I am not laughing at you . . .

THE MANAGER (*to Step-Daughter*). You ought to feel honoured to be played by . . .

LEADING LADY (*at once, contemptuously*). "That woman there" . . .

THE STEP-DAUGHTER. But I wasn't speaking of you, you know. I was speaking of myself—whom I can't see at all in you! That is all. I don't know . . . but . . . you . . . aren't in the least like me . . .

THE FATHER. True. Here's the point. Look here, sir, our temperaments, our souls . . .

THE MANAGER. Temperament, soul, be hanged! Do you suppose the spirit of the piece is in you? Nothing of the kind!

THE FATHER. What, haven't we our own temperaments, our own souls?

THE MANAGER. Not at all. Your soul or whatever you like to call it takes shape here. The actors give body and form to it, voice and gesture. And my actors—I may tell you—have given expression to much more lofty material than this little drama of yours, which may or may not hold up on the stage. But if it does, the merit of it, believe me, will be due to my actors.

THE FATHER. I don't dare contradict you, sir; but, believe me, it is a terrible suffering for us who are as we are, with these bodies of ours, these features to see . . .

THE MANAGER (*cutting him short and out of patience*). Good heavens! The make-up will remedy all that, man, the make-up . . .

THE FATHER. Maybe. But the voice, the gestures . . .

THE MANAGER. Now, look here! On the stage, you as yourself, cannot exist. The actor here acts you, and that's an end to it!

THE FATHER. I understand. And now I think I see why our author who conceived us as we are, all alive, didn't want to put us on the stage after all. I haven't the least desire to offend your actors. Far from it! But when I think that I am to be acted by . . . I don't know by whom . . .

LEADING MAN (*on his dignity*). By me, if you've no objection!

THE FATHER (*humbly, mellifluously*). Honoured, I assure you, sir. (*Bows*). Still, I must say that try as this gentleman may, with all his good will and wonderful art, to absorb me into himself . . .

LEADING MAN. Oh chuck it! "Wonderful art!" Withdraw that, please!

THE FATHER. The performance he will give, even doing his best with make-up to look like me . . .

LEADING MAN. It will certainly be a bit difficult! (*The actors laugh.*)

THE FATHER. Exactly! It will be difficult to act me as I really am. The effect will be rather—apart from the make-up—according as to how he supposes I am, as he senses me—if he does sense me—and not as I inside of myself feel myself to be. It seems to me then that account should be taken of this by everyone whose duty it may become to criticize us . . .

THE MANAGER. Heavens! The man's starting to think about the critics now! Let them say what they like. It's up to us to put on the play if we can (*looking around*). Come on! come on! Is the stage set? (*To the actors and Characters*): Stand back—stand back! Let me see, and don't let's lose any more time! (*To the Step-Daughter*): Is it all right as it is now?

THE STEP-DAUGHTER. Well, to tell the truth, I don't recognize the scene.

THE MANAGER. My dear lady, you can't possibly suppose that we can construct that shop of Madame Pace piece by piece here? (*To the Father*): You said a white room with flowered wall paper, didn't you?

THE FATHER. Yes.

THE MANAGER. Well then. We've got the furniture right more or less. Bring that little table a bit further forward. (*The stage hands obey the order. To Property Man*): You go and find an envelope, if possible, a pale blue one; and give it to that gentleman (*indicates Father*).

PROPERTY MAN. An ordinary envelope?

MANAGER *and* FATHER. Yes, yes, an ordinary envelope.

PROPERTY MAN. At once, sir (*exit*).

THE MANAGER. Ready, everyone! First scene—the Young Lady. (*The Leading Lady comes forward*). No, no, you must wait. I meant her (*indicating the Step-Daughter*). You just watch—

THE STEP-DAUGHTER (*adding at once*). How I shall play it, how I shall live it! . . .

LEADING LADY (*offended*). I shall live it also, you may be sure, as soon as I begin!

THE MANAGER (*with his hands to his head*). Ladies and gentlemen, if you please! No more useless discussions! Scene I: the young lady with Madame Pace: Oh! (*looks around as if lost*). And this Madame Pace, where is she?

THE FATHER. She isn't with us, sir.

THE MANAGER. Then what the devil's to be done?

THE FATHER. But she is alive too.

THE MANAGER. Yes, but where is she?

THE FATHER. One minute. Let me speak! (*turning to the actresses*). If these ladies would be so good as to give me their hats for a moment . . .

THE ACTRESSES (*half surprised, half laughing, in chorus*). What?

Why?

Our hats?

What does he say?

THE MANAGER. What are you going to do with the ladies' hats? (*The actors laugh*).

THE FATHER. Oh nothing. I just want to put them on these pegs for a moment. And one of the ladies will be so kind as to take off her mantle . . .

THE ACTORS. Oh, what d'you think of that?

Only the mantle?

He must be mad.

SOME ACTRESSES. But why?

Mantles as well?

THE FATHER. To hang them up here for a moment. Please be so kind, will you?

The Actresses (*taking off their hats, one or two also their cloaks, and going to hang them on the racks*). After all, why not?
There you are!
This is really funny.
We've got to put them on show.
The Father. Exactly; just like that, on show.
The Manager. May we know why?
The Father. I'll tell you. Who knows if, by arranging the stage for her, she does not come here herself, attracted by the very articles of her trade? (*Inviting the actors to look towards the exit at back of stage*): Look! Look!

(*The door at the back of stage opens and* Madame Pace *enters and takes a few steps forward. She is a fat, oldish woman with puffy oxygenated hair. She is rouged and powdered, dressed with a comical elegance in black silk. Round her waist is a long silver chain from which hangs a pair of scissors. The Step-Daughter runs over to her at once amid the stupor of the actors*).

The Step-Daughter (*turning towards her*). There she is! There she is!
The Father (*radiant*). It's she! I said so, didn't I? There she is!
The Manager (*conquering his surprise, and then becoming indignant*). What sort of a trick is this?
Leading Man (*almost at the same time*). What's going to happen next?
Juvenile Lead. Where does *she* come from?
L'Ingénue. They've been holding her in reserve, I guess.
Leading Lady. A vulgar trick!
The Father (*dominating the protests*). Excuse me, all of you! Why are you so anxious to destroy in the name

of a vulgar, commonplace sense of truth, this reality which comes to birth attracted and formed by the magic of the stage itself, which has indeed more right to live here than you, since it is much truer than you—if you don't mind my saying so? Which is the actress among you who is to play Madame Pace? Well, here is Madame Pace herself. And you will allow, I fancy, that the actress who acts her will be less true than this woman here, who is herself in person. You see my daughter recognized her and went over to her at once. Now you're going to witness the scene!

But the scene between the STEP-DAUGHTER *and* MADAME PACE *has already begun despite the protest of the actors and the reply of* THE FATHER. *It has begun quietly, naturally, in a manner impossible for the stage. So when the actors, called to attention by* THE FATHER, *turn round and see* MADAME PACE, *who has placed one hand under the* STEP-DAUGHTER'S *chin to raise her head, they observe her at first with great attention, but hearing her speak in an unintelligible manner their interest begins to wane.*

THE MANAGER. Well? well?

LEADING MAN. What does she say?

LEADING LADY. One can't hear a word.

JUVENILE LEAD. Louder! Louder please!

THE STEP-DAUGHTER (*leaving Madame Pace, who smiles a Sphinx-like smile, and advancing towards the actors*). Louder? Louder? What are you talking about? These aren't matters which can be shouted at the top of one's voice. If I have spoken them out loud, it was to shame him and have my revenge (*indicates Father*). But for Madame it's quite a different matter.

THE MANAGER. Indeed? indeed? But here, you know, people have got to make themselves heard, my dear. Even we who are on the stage can't hear you. What will it be when the public's in the theatre? And anyway, you can very well speak up now among yourselves, since we shan't be present to listen to you as we are now. You've got to pretend to be alone in a room at the back of a shop where no one can hear you.

(THE STEP-DAUGHTER *coquettishly and with a touch of malice makes a sign of disagreement two or three times with her finger*).

THE MANAGER. What do you mean by no?

THE STEP-DAUGHTER (*sotto voce, mysteriously*). There's someone who will hear us if she (*indicating Madame Pace*) speaks out loud.

THE MANAGER (*in consternation*). What? Have you got someone else to spring on us now? (*The actors burst out laughing*).

THE FATHER. No, no sir. She is alluding to me. I've got to be here—there behind that door, in waiting; and Madame Pace knows it. In fact, if you will allow me, I'll go there at once, so I can be quite ready. (*Moves away*).

THE MANAGER (*stopping him*). No! Wait! wait! We must observe the conventions of the theatre. Before you are ready . . .

THE STEP-DAUGHTER (*interrupting him*). No, get on with it at once! I'm just dying, I tell you, to act this scene. If he's ready, I'm more than ready.

THE MANAGER (*shouting*). But, my dear young lady, first of all, we must have the scene between you and this lady . . . (*indicates Madame Pace*). Do you understand? . . .

THE STEP-DAUGHTER. Good Heavens! She's been telling me what you know already: that mamma's work is badly done again, that the material's ruined; and that if I want her to continue to help us in our misery I must be patient . . .

MADAME PACE (*coming forward with an air of great im-*

portance). Yes indeed, sir, I no wanta take advantage of her, I no wanta be hard . . .

(*Note. Madame Pace is supposed to talk in a jargon half Italian, half Spanish*).

THE MANAGER (*alarmed*). What? What? She talks like that? (*The actors burst out laughing again*).

THE STEP-DAUGHTER (*also laughing*). Yes yes, that's the way she talks, half English, half Italian! Most comical it is!

MADAME PACE. Itta seem not verra polite gentlemen laugha atta me eef I trya best speaka English.

THE MANAGER. *Diamine!* Of course! Of course! Let her talk like that! Just what we want. Talk just like that, Madam, if you please! The effect will be certain. Exactly what was wanted to put a little comic relief into the crudity of the situation. Of course she talks like that! Magnificent!

THE STEP-DAUGHTER. Magnificent? Certainly! When certain suggestions are made to one in language of that kind, the effect is certain, since it seems almost a joke. One feels inclined to laugh when one hears her talk about an "old signore" "who wanta talka nicely with you." Nice old signore, eh, Madame?

MADAME PACE. Not so old my dear, not so old! And even if you no lika him, he won't make any scandal!

THE MOTHER (*jumping up amid the amazement and consternation of the actors who had not been noticing her. They move to restrain her*). You old devil! You murderess!

THE STEP-DAUGHTER (*running over to calm her Mother*). Calm yourself, mother, calm yourself! Please don't . . .

THE FATHER (*going to her also at the same time*). Calm yourself! Don't get excited! Sit down now!

THE MOTHER. Well then, take that woman away out of my sight!

THE STEP-DAUGHTER (*to Manager*). It is impossible for my mother to remain here.

THE FATHER (*to Manager*). They can't be here together. And for this reason, you see: that woman there was not with us when we came . . . If they are on together, the whole thing is given away inevitably, as you see.

THE MANAGER. It doesn't matter. This is only a first rough sketch—just to get an idea of the various points of the scene, even confusedly . . . (*Turning to the Mother and leading her to her chair*): Come along, my dear lady, sit down now, and let's get on with the scene . . .

(*Meanwhile, the* STEP-DAUGHTER, *coming forward again, turns to Madame Pace*).

THE STEP-DAUGHTER. Come on, Madame, come on!

MADAME PACE (*offended*). No, no, *grazie*. I not do anything witha your mother present.

THE STEP-DAUGHTER. Nonsense! Introduce this "old signore" who wants to talk nicely to me (*addressing the company imperiously*). We've got to do this scene one way or another, haven't we? Come on! (*to Madame Pace*). You can go!

MADAME PACE. Ah yes! I go'way! I go'way! Certainly! (*Exist furious*).

THE STEP-DAUGHTER (*to the Father*). Now you make your entry. No, you needn't go over here. Come here. Let's suppose you've already come in. Like that, yes! I'm here with bowed head, modest like. Come on! Out with your voice! Say "Good morning, Miss" in that peculiar tone, that special tone . . .

THE MANAGER. Excuse me, but are you the Manager, or am I? (*To the Father, who looks undecided and perplexed*): Get on with it, man! Go down there to the back of the stage. You needn't go off. Then come right forward here.

[Act II] SIX CHARACTERS 45

(THE FATHER *does as he is told, looking troubled and perplexed at first. But as soon as he begins to move, the reality of the action affects him, and he begins to smile and to be more natural. The actors watch intently*).

THE MANAGER (*sottovoce, quickly to the Prompter in his box*). Ready! ready? Get ready to write now.

THE FATHER (*coming forward and speaking in a different tone*). Good afternoon, Miss!

THE STEP-DAUGHTER (*head bowed down slightly, with restrained disgust*). Good afternoon!

THE FATHER (*looks under her hat which partly covers her face. Perceiving she is very young, he makes an exclamation, partly of surprise, partly of fear lest he compromise himself in a risky adventure*) Ah . . . but . . . ah . . . I say . . . this is not the first time that you have come here, is it?

THE STEP-DAUGHTER (*modestly*). No sir.

THE FATHER. You've been here before, eh? (*Then seeing her nod agreement*): More than once? (*Waits for her to answer, looks under her hat, smiles, and then says*): Well then, there's no need to be so shy, is there? May I take off your hat?

THE STEP-DAUGHTER (*anticipating him and with veiled disgust*). No sir . . . I'll do it myself. (*Takes it off quickly*).

(THE MOTHER, *who watches the progress of the scene with* THE SON *and the other two children who cling to her, is on thorns; and follows with varying expressions of sorrow, indignation, anxiety, and horror the words and actions of the other two. From time to time she hides her face in her hands and sobs*).

THE MOTHER. Oh, my God, my God!

THE FATHER (*playing his part with a touch of gallantry*). Give it to me! I'll put it down (*takes hat from her hands*).

But a dear little head like yours ought to have a smarter hat. Come and help me choose one from the stock, won't you?

L'Ingénue (*interrupting*). I say ... those are our hats you know.

The Manager (*furious*). Silence! silence! Don't try and be funny, if you please ... We're playing the scene now I'd have you notice. (*To the Step-Daughter*). Begin again, please!

The Step-Daughter (*continuing*). No thank you, sir.

The Father. Oh, come now. Don't talk like that. You must take it. I shall be upset if you don't. There are some lovely little hats here; and then—Madame will be pleased. She expects it, anyway, you know.

The Step-Daughter. No, no! I couldn't wear it!

The Father. Oh, you're thinking about what they'd say at home if they saw you come in with a new hat? My dear girl, there's always a way round these little matters, you know.

The Step-Daughter (*all keyed up*). No, it's not that. I couldn't wear it because I am ... as you see ... you might have noticed ... (*showing her black dress*).

The Father. ... in mourning! Of course: I beg your pardon: I'm frightfully sorry ...

The Step-Daughter (*forcing herself to conquer her indignation and nausea*). Stop! Stop! It's I who must thank you. There's no need for you to feel mortified or specially sorry. Don't think any more of what I've said. (*Tries to smile*). I must forget that I am dressed so ...

The Manager (*interrupting and turning to the Prompter*). Stop a minute! Stop! Don't write that down. Cut out that last bit. (*Then to the Father and Step-Daughter*). Fine! it's going fine! (*To the Father only*). And now you can go on as we arranged. (*To the actors*). Pretty good that scene, where he offers her the hat, eh?

The Step-Daughter. The best's coming now. Why can't we go on?

The Manager. Have a little patience! (*To the actors*): Of course, it must be treated rather lightly.

Leading Man. Still, with a bit of go in it!

Leading Lady. Of course! It's easy enough! (*To Leading Man*): Shall you and I try it now?

Leading Man. Why, yes! I'll prepare my entrance. (*Exit in order to make his entrance*).

The Manager (*to Leading Lady*). See here! The scene between you and Madame Pace is finished. I'll have it written out properly after. You remain here . . . oh, where are you going?

Leading Lady. One minute. I want to put my hat on again (*goes over to hat-rack and puts her hat on her head*).

The Manager. Good! You stay here with your head bowed down a bit.

The Step-Daughter. But she isn't dressed in black.

Leading Lady. But I shall be, and much more effectively than you.

The Manager (*to Step-Daughter*). Be quiet please, and watch! You'll be able to learn something. (*Clapping his hands*) Come on! come on! Entrance, please!

(*The door at rear of stage opens, and the Leading Man enters with the lively manner of an old gallant. The rendering of the scene by the actors from the very first words is seen to be quite a different thing, though it has not in any way the air of a parody. Naturally, the Step-Daughter and the Father, not being able to recognize themselves in the Leading Lady and the Leading Man, who deliver their words in different tones and with a different psychology, express, sometimes with smiles, sometimes with gestures, the impression they receive*).

Leading Man. Good afternoon, Miss . . .

THE FATHER (*at once unable to contain himself*). No! no!

(THE STEP-DAUGHTER *noticing the way the* LEADING MAN *enters, bursts out laughing*).

THE MANAGER (*furious*). Silence! And you please just stop that laughing. If we go on like this, we shall never finish.

THE STEP-DAUGHTER. Forgive me, sir, but it's natural enough. This lady (*indicating Leading Lady*) stands there still; but if she is supposed to be me, I can assure you that if I heard anyone say "Good afternoon" in that manner and in that tone, I should burst out laughing as I did.

THE FATHER. Yes, yes, the manner, the tone . . .

THE MANAGER. Nonsense! Rubbish! Stand aside and let me see the action.

LEADING MAN. If I've got to represent an old fellow who's coming into a house of an equivocal character . . .

THE MANAGER. Don't listen to them, for Heaven's sake! Do it again! It goes fine. (*Waiting for the actors to begin again*): Well?

LEADING MAN. Good afternoon, Miss.

LEADING LADY. Good afternoon.

LEADING MAN (*imitating the gesture of the Father when he looked under the hat, and then expressing quite clearly first satisfaction and then fear*). Ah, but . . . I say . . . this is not the first time that you have come here, is it?

THE MANAGER. Good, but not quite so heavily. Like this (*acts himself*): "This isn't the first time that you have come here" . . . (*To Leading Lady*) And you say: "No, sir."

LEADING LADY. No, sir.

LEADING MAN. You've been here before, more than once.

THE MANAGER. No, no, stop! Let her nod "yes" first.

"You've been here before, eh?" (*The Leading Lady lifts up her head slightly and closes her eyes as though in disgust. Then she inclines her head twice*).

THE STEP-DAUGHTER (*unable to contain herself*). Oh my God! (*Puts a hand to her mouth to prevent herself from laughing*).

THE MANAGER (*turning round*). What's the matter?

THE STEP-DAUGHTER. Nothing, nothing!

THE MANAGER (*to Leading Man*). Go on!

LEADING MAN. You've been here before, eh? Well then, there's no need to be so shy, is there? May I take off your hat?

(THE LEADING MAN *says this last speech in such a tone and with such gestures that the* STEP-DAUGHTER, *though she has her hand to her mouth, cannot keep from laughing*).

LEADING LADY (*indignant*). I'm not going to stop here to be made a fool of by that woman there.

LEADING MAN. Neither am I! I'm through with it!

THE MANAGER (*shouting to Step-Daughter*). Silence! for once and all, I tell you!

THE STEP-DAUGHTER. Forgive me! forgive me!

THE MANAGER. You haven't any manners: that's what it is! You go too far.

THE FATHER (*endeavouring to intervene*). Yes, it's true, but excuse her . . .

THE MANAGER. Excuse what? It's absolutely disgusting.

THE FATHER. Yes, sir, but believe me, it has such a strange effect when . . .

THE MANAGER. Strange? Why strange? Where is it strange?

THE FATHER. No, sir; I admire your actors—this gentleman here, this lady; but they are certainly not us!

THE MANAGER. I should hope not. Evidently they cannot be you, if they are actors.

THE FATHER. Just so: actors! Both of them act our parts exceedingly well. But, believe me, it produces quite a different effect on us. They want to be us, but they aren't, all the same.

THE MANAGER. What is it then anyway?

THE FATHER. Something that is . . . that is theirs—and no longer ours . . .

THE MANAGER. But naturally, inevitably. I've told you so already.

THE FATHER. Yes, I understand . . . I understand . . .

THE MANAGER. Well then, let's have no more of it! (*Turning to the actors*): We'll have the rehearsals by ourselves, afterwards, in the ordinary way. I never could stand rehearsing with the author present. He's never satisfied! (*Turning to Father and Step-Daughter*): Come on! Let's get on with it again; and try and see if you can't keep from laughing.

THE STEP-DAUGHTER. Oh, I shan't laugh any more. There's a nice little bit coming for me now: you'll see.

THE MANAGER. Well then: when she says "Don't think any more of what I've said. I must forget, etc.," you (*addressing the Father*) come in sharp with "I understand, I understand"; and then you ask her . . .

THE STEP-DAUGHTER (*interrupting*). What?

THE MANAGER. Why she is in mourning.

THE STEP-DAUGHTER. Not at all! See here: when I told him that it was useless for me to be thinking about my wearing mourning, do you know how he answered me? "Ah well," he said "then let's take off this little frock."

THE MANAGER. Great! Just what we want, to make a riot in the theatre!

THE STEP-DAUGHTER. But it's the truth!

THE MANAGER. What does that matter? Acting is our business here. Truth up to a certain point, but no further.

THE STEP-DAUGHTER. What do you want to do then?

THE MANAGER. You'll see, you'll see! Leave it to me.

THE STEP-DAUGHTER. No sir! What you want to do is to piece together a little romantic sentimental scene out of my disgust, out of all the reasons, each more cruel and viler than the other, why I am what I am. He is to ask me why I'm in mourning; and I'm to answer with tears in my eyes, that it is just two months since papa died. No sir, no! He's got to say to me; as he did say: "Well, let's take off this little dress at once." And I; with my two months' mourning in my heart, went there behind that screen, and with these fingers tingling with shame . . .

THE MANAGER (*running his hands through his hair*). For Heaven's sake! What are you saying?

THE STEP-DAUGHTER (*crying out excitedly*). The truth! The truth!

THE MANAGER. It may be. I don't deny it, and I can understand all your horror; but you must surely see that you can't have this kind of thing on the stage. It won't go.

THE STEP-DAUGHTER. Not possible, eh? Very well! I'm much obliged to you—but I'm off!

THE MANAGER. Now be reasonable! Don't lose your temper!

THE STEP-DAUGHTER. I won't stop here! I won't! I can see you've fixed it all up with him in your office. All this talk about what is possible for the stage . . . I understand! He wants to get at his complicated "cerebral drama," to have his famous remorses and torments acted; but I want to act my part, *my part!*

THE MANAGER (*annoyed, shaking his shoulders*). Ah! Just *your* part! But, if you will pardon me, there are other parts than yours: His (*indicating the Father*) and hers (*in-*

dicating the Mother)! On the stage you can't have a character becoming too prominent and overshadowing all the others. The thing is to pack them all into a neat little framework and then act what is actable. I am aware of the fact that everyone has his own interior life which he wants very much to put forward. But the difficulty lies in this fact: to set out just so much as is necessary for the stage, taking the other characters into consideration, and at the same time hint at the unrevealed interior life of each. I am willing to admit, my dear young lady, that from your point of view it would be a fine idea if each character could tell the public all his troubles in a nice monologue or a regular one hour lecture (*good humoredly*). You must restrain yourself, my dear, and in your own interest, too; because this fury of yours, this exaggerated disgust you show, may make a bad impression, you know. After you have confessed to me that there were others before him at Madame Pace's and more than once . . .

THE STEP-DAUGHTER (*bowing her head, impressed*). It's true. But remember those others mean him for me all the same.

THE MANAGER (*not understanding*). What? The others? What do you mean?

THE STEP-DAUGHTER. For one who has gone wrong, sir, he who was responsible for the first fault is responsible for all that follow. He is responsible for my faults, was, even before I was born. Look at him, and see if it isn't true!

THE MANAGER. Well, well! And does the weight of so much responsibility seem nothing to you? Give him a chance to act it, to get it over!

THE STEP-DAUGHTER. How? How can he act all his "noble remorses" all his "moral torments," if you want to spare him the horror of being discovered one day—after he had asked her what he did ask her—in the arms of her, that already fallen woman, that child, sir, that child he used to watch come out of school? (*She is moved*).

(THE MOTHER *at this point is overcome with emotion, and breaks out into a fit of crying. All are touched. A long pause*).

THE STEP-DAUGHTER (*as soon as the Mother becomes a little quieter, adds resolutely and gravely*). At present, we are unknown to the public. Tomorrow, you will act us as you wish, treating us in your own manner. But do you really want to see drama, do you want to see it flash out as it really did?

THE MANAGER. Of course! That's just what I do want, so I can use as much of it as is possible.

THE STEP-DAUGHTER. Well then, ask that Mother there to leave us.

THE MOTHER (*changing her low plaint into a sharp cry*). No! No! Don't permit it, sir, don't permit it!

THE MANAGER. But it's only to try it.

THE MOTHER. I can't bear it. I can't.

THE MANAGER. But since it has happened already . . . I don't understand!

THE MOTHER. It's taking place now. It happens all the time. My torment isn't a pretended one. I live and feel every minute of my torture. Those two children there—have you heard them speak? They can't speak any more. They cling to me to keep my torment actual and vivid for me. But for themselves, they do not exist, they aren't any more. And she (*indicating Step-Daughter*) has run away, she has left me, and is lost. If I now see her here before me, it is only to renew for me the tortures I have suffered for her too.

THE FATHER. The eternal moment! She (*indicating the Step-Daughter*) is here to catch me, fix me, and hold me eternally in the stocks for that one fleeting and shameful moment of my life. She can't give it up! And you sir, cannot either fairly spare me it.

THE MANAGER. I never said I didn't want to act it. It will form, as a matter of fact, the nucleus of the whole first act right up to her surprise (*indicates the Mother*).

THE FATHER. Just so! This is my punishment: the passion in all of us that must culminate in her final cry.

THE STEP-DAUGHTER. I can hear it still in my ears. It's driven me mad, that cry!—You can put me on as you like; it doesn't matter. Fully dressed, if you like—provided I have at least the arm bare; because, standing like this (*she goes close to the Father and leans her head on his breast*) with my head so, and my arms round his neck, I saw a vein pulsing in my arm here; and then, as if that live vein had awakened disgust in me, I closed my eyes like this, and let my head sink on his breast. (*Turning to the Mother*). Cry out mother! Cry out! (*Buries head in Father's breast, and with her shoulders raised as if to prevent her hearing the cry, adds in tones of intense emotion*): Cry out as you did then!

THE MOTHER (*coming forward to separate them*). No! My daughter, my daughter! (*And after having pulled her away from him*): You brute! you brute! She is my daughter! Don't you see she's my daughter?

THE MANAGER (*walking backwards towards footlights*). Fine! fine! Damned good! And then, of course—curtain!

THE FATHER (*going towards him excitedly*). Yes, of course, because that's the way it really happened.

THE MANAGER (*convinced and pleased*). Oh, yes, no doubt about it. Curtain here, curtain!

(*At the reiterated cry of* THE MANAGER, *THE MACHINIST lets the curtain down, leaving* THE MANAGER *and* THE FATHER *in front of it before the footlights*).

THE MANAGER. The darned idiot! I said "curtain" to

show the act should end there, and he goes and lets it down in earnest (*to the Father, while he pulls the curtain back to go on to the stage again*). Yes, yes, it's all right. Effect certain! That's the right ending. I'll guarantee the first act at any rate.

ACT III.

When the curtain goes up again, it is seen that the stage hands have shifted the bit of scenery used in the last part, and have rigged up instead at the back of the stage a drop, with some trees, and one or two wings. A portion of a fountain basin is visible. The Mother is sitting on the Right with the two children by her side. The Son is on the same side, but away from the others. He seems bored, angry, and full of shame. The Father and The Step-Daughter are also seated towards the Right front. On the other side (Left) are the actors, much in the positions they occupied before the curtain was lowered. Only the Manager is standing up in the middle of the stage, with his hand closed over his mouth in the act of meditating.

THE MANAGER (*shaking his shoulders after a brief pause*). Ah yes: the second act! Leave it to me, leave it all to me as we arranged, and you'll see! It'll go fine!

THE STEP-DAUGHTER. Our entry into his house (*indicates Father*) in spite of him (*indicates the Son*) . . .

THE MANAGER (*out of patience*). Leave it to me, I tell you!

THE STEP-DAUGHTER. Do let it be clear, at any rate, that it is in spite of my wishes.

THE MOTHER (*from her corner, shaking her head*). For all the good that's come of it . . .

THE STEP-DAUGHTER (*turning towards her quickly*). It doesn't matter. The more harm done us, the more remorse for him.

THE MANAGER (*impatiently*). I understand! Good Heavens! I understand! I'm taking it into account.

THE MOTHER (*supplicatingly*). I beg you, sir, to let it appear quite plain that for conscience sake I did try in every way . . .

THE STEP-DAUGHTER (*interrupting indignantly and continuing for the Mother*). . . . to pacify me, to dissuade me from spiting him. (*To Manager*). Do as she wants: satisfy her, because it is true! I enjoy it immensely. Anyhow, as you can see, the meeker she is, the more she tries to get at his heart, the more distant and aloof does he become.

THE MANAGER. Are we going to begin this second act or not?

THE STEP-DAUGHTER. I'm not going to talk any more now. But I must tell you this: you can't have the whole action take place in the garden, as you suggest. It isn't possible!

THE MANAGER. Why not?

THE STEP-DAUGHTER. Because he (*indicates the Son again*) is always shut up alone in his room. And then there's all the part of that poor dazed-looking boy there which takes place indoors.

THE MANAGER. Maybe! On the other hand, you will understand—we can't change scenes three or four times in one act.

THE LEADING MAN. They used to once.

THE MANAGER. Yes, when the public was up to the level of that child there.

THE LEADING LADY. It makes the illusion easier.

THE FATHER (*irritated*). The illusion! For Heaven's sake, don't say illusion. Please don't use that word, which is particularly painful for us.

THE MANAGER (*astounded*). And why, if you please?

THE FATHER. It's painful, cruel, really cruel; and you ought to understand that.

THE MANAGER. But why? What ought we to say

then? The illusion, I tell you, sir, which we've got to create for the audience . . .

THE LEADING MAN. With our acting.

THE MANAGER. The illusion of a reality.

THE FATHER. I understand; but you, perhaps, do not understand us. Forgive me! You see . . . here for you and your actors, the thing is only—and rightly so . . . a kind of game . . .

THE LEADING LADY (*interrupting indignantly*). A game! We're not children here, if you please! We are serious actors.

THE FATHER. I don't deny it. What I mean is the game, or play, of your art, which has to give, as the gentleman says, a perfect illusion of reality.

THE MANAGER. Precisely—!

THE FATHER. Now, if you consider the fact that we (*indicates himself and the other five Characters*), as we are, have no other reality outside of this illusion . . .

THE MANAGER (*astonished, looking at his actors, who are also amazed*). And what does that mean?

THE FATHER (*after watching them for a moment with a wan smile*). As I say, sir, that which is a game of art for you is our sole reality. (*Brief pause. He goes a step or two nearer the Manager and adds*): But not only for us, you know, by the way. Just you think it over well. (*Looks him in the eyes*). Can you tell me who you are?

THE MANAGER (*perplexed, half smiling*). What? Who am I? I am myself.

THE FATHER. And if I were to tell you that that isn't true, because you are I . . . ?

THE MANAGER. I should say you were mad—! (*The actors laugh*).

THE FATHER. You're quite right to laugh: because we are all making believe here (*to Manager*). And you can therefore object that it's only for a joke that that gentleman there (*indicates the Leading Man*), who naturally is himself, has to be me, who am on the contrary myself—this thing you see here. You see I've caught you in a trap! (*The actors laugh*).

THE MANAGER (*annoyed*). But we've had all this over once before. Do you want to begin again?

THE FATHER. No, no! That wasn't my meaning! In fact, I should like to request you to abandon this game of art (*looking at the Leading Lady as if anticipating her*) which you are accustomed to play here with your actors, and to ask you seriously once again: who are you?

THE MANAGER (*astonished and irritated, turning to his actors*). If this fellow here hasn't got a nerve! A man who calls himself a character comes and asks me who I am!

THE FATHER (*with dignity, but not offended*). A character, sir, may always asks a man who he is. Because a character has really a life of his own, marked with his especial characteristics; for which reason he is always "somebody." But a man—I'm not speaking of you now—may very well be "nobody."

THE MANAGER. Yes, but you are asking these questions of me, the boss, the manager! Do you understand?

THE FATHER. But only in order to know if you, as you really are now, see yourself as you once were with all the illusions that were yours then, with all the things both inside and outside of you as they seemed to you—as they were then indeed for you. Well, sir, if you think of all those illusions that mean nothing to you now, of all those things which don't even *seem* to you to exist any more, while once they *were* for you, don't you feel that—I won't say these boards—but the very earth under your feet is sinking away from you when you reflect that in the same way this *you* as you feel it today—all this present reality of yours—is fated to seem a mere illusion to you tomorrow?

THE MANAGER (*without having understood much, but astonished by the specious argument*). Well, well! And where does all this take us anyway?

THE FATHER. Oh, nowhere! It's only to show you that if we (*indicating the Characters*) have no other reality beyond the illusion, you too must not count overmuch on your reality as you feel it today, since, like that of yesterday, it may prove an illusion for you tomorrow.

THE MANAGER (*determining to make fun of him*). Ah, excellent! Then you'll be saying next that you, with this comedy of yours that you brought here to act, are truer and more real than I am.

THE FATHER (*with the greatest seriousness*). But of course; without doubt!

THE MANAGER. Ah, really?

THE FATHER. Why, I thought you'd understand that from the beginning.

THE MANAGER. More real than I?

THE FATHER. If your reality can change from one day to another . . .

THE MANAGER. But everyone knows it can change. It is always changing, the same as anyone else's.

THE FATHER (*with a cry*). No, sir, not ours! Look here! That is the very difference! Our reality doesn't change: it can't change! It can't be other than what it is, because it is already fixed for ever. It's terrible. Ours is an immutable reality which should make you shudder when you approach us if you are really conscious of the fact that your reality is a mere transitory and fleeting illusion, taking this form today and that tomorrow, according to the conditions, according to your will, your sentiments, which in turn are controlled by an intellect that shows them to you today in one manner and tomorrow . . . who knows how? . . . Illusions of reality represented in this fatuous comedy of life that never ends, nor can ever end! Because if tomorrow it were to end . . . then why, all would be finished.

THE MANAGER. Oh for God's sake, will you *at least* finish with this philosophizing and let us try and shape this comedy which you yourself have brought me here? You argue and philosophize a bit too much, my dear sir. You know you seem to me almost, almost . . . (*Stops and looks him over from head to foot*). Ah, by the way, I think you introduced yourself to me as a—what shall . . . we say— a "character," created by an author who did not afterward care to make a drama of his own creations.

THE FATHER. It is the simple truth, sir.

THE MANAGER. Nonsense! Cut that out, please! None of us believes it, because it isn't a thing, as you must recognize yourself, which one can believe seriously. If you want to know, it seems to me you are trying to imitate the manner of a certain author whom I heartily detest—I warn you— although I have unfortunately bound myself to put on one of his works. As a matter of fact, I was just starting to rehearse it, when you arrived. (*Turning to the actors*): And this is what we've gained—out of the frying-pan into the fire!

THE FATHER. I don't know to what author you may be alluding, but believe me I feel what I think; and I seem to be philosophizing only for those who do not think what they feel, because they blind themselves with their own sentiment. I know that for many people this self-blinding seems much more "human"; but the contrary is really true. For man never reasons so much and becomes so introspective as when he suffers; since he is anxious to get at the cause of his sufferings, to learn who has produced them, and whether it is just or unjust that he should have to bear them. On the other hand, when he is happy, he takes his happiness as it comes and doesn't analyse it, just as if happiness were his right. The animals suffer without reasoning about their sufferings. But take the case of a man who suffers and begins to reason about it. Oh no! it can't be allowed! Let him suffer like an animal, and then—ah yes, he is "human!"

THE MANAGER. Look here! Look here! You're off again, philosophizing worse than ever.

THE FATHER. Because I suffer, sir! I'm not philosophizing: I'm crying aloud the reason of my sufferings.

THE MANAGER (*makes brusque movement as he is taken with a new idea*). I should like to know if anyone has ever heard of a character who gets right out of his part and perorates and speechifies as you do. Have you ever heard of a case? I haven't.

THE FATHER. You have never met such a case, sir, because authors, as a rule, hide the labour of their creations. When the characters are really alive before their author, the latter does nothing but follow them in their action, in their words, in the situations which they suggest to him; and he has to will them the way they will themselves—for there's trouble if he doesn't. When a character is born, he acquires at once such an independence, even of his own author, that he can be imagined by everybody even in many other situations where the author never dreamed of placing him; and so he acquires for himself a meaning which the author never thought of giving him.

THE MANAGER. Yes, yes, I know this.

THE FATHER. What is there then to marvel at in us? Imagine such a misfortune for characters as I have described to you: to be born of an author's fantasy, and be denied life by him; and then answer me if these characters left alive, and yet without life, weren't right in doing what they did do and are doing now, after they have attempted everything in their power to persuade him to give them their stage life. We've all tried him in turn, I, she (*indicating the Step-Daughter*) and she (*indicating the Mother*).

THE STEP-DAUGHTER. It's true. I too have sought to tempt him, many, many times, when he has been sitting at his writing table, feeling a bit melancholy, at the twilight hour. He would sit in his armchair too lazy to switch on the light, and all the shadows that crept into his room were full of our presence coming to tempt him. (*As if she saw herself still there by the writing table, and was annoyed by the presence of the actors*): Oh, if you would only go away, go away and leave us alone—mother here with that son of hers—I with that Child—that Boy there always alone —and then I with him (*just hints at the Father*)—and then I alone, alone . . . in those shadows! (*Makes a sudden movement as if in the vision she has of herself illuminating those shadows she wanted to seize hold of herself*). Ah! my life! my life! Oh, what scenes we proposed to him—and I tempted him more than any of the others!

THE FATHER. Maybe. But perhaps it was your fault that he refused to give us life: because you were too insistent, too troublesome.

THE STEP-DAUGHTER. Nonsense! Didn't he make me so himself? (*Goes close to the Manager to tell him as if in confidence*). In my opinion he abandoned us in a fit of depression, of disgust for the ordinary theatre as the public knows it and likes it.

THE SON. Exactly what it was, sir; exactly that!

THE FATHER. Not at all! Don't believe it for a minute. Listen to me! You'll be doing quite right to modify, as you suggest, the excesses both of this girl here, who wants to do too much, and of this young man, who won't do anything at all.

THE SON. No, nothing!

THE MANAGER. You too get over the mark occasionally, my dear sir, if I may say so.

THE FATHER. I? When? Where?

THE MANAGER. Always! Continuously! Then there's this insistence of yours in trying to make us believe you are a character. And then too, you must really argue and philosophize less, you know, much less.

THE FATHER. Well, if you want to take away from me the possibility of representing the torment of my spirit which never gives me peace, you will be suppressing me: that's all. Every true man, sir, who is a little above the level of the beasts and plants does not live for the sake of living, without knowing how to live; but he lives so as to give a meaning and a value of his own to life. For me this is *everything*. I cannot give up this, just to represent a mere fact as she (*indicating the Step-Daughter*) wants. It's all very well for her, since her "vendetta" lies in the "fact." I'm not going to do it. It destroys my *raison d'être*.

THE MANAGER. Your *raison d'être!* Oh, we're going ahead fine! First she starts off, and then you jump in. At this rate, we'll never finish.

THE FATHER. Now, don't be offended! Have it your own way—provided, however, that within the limits of the parts you assign us each one's sacrifice isn't too great.

THE MANAGER. You've got to understand that you can't go on arguing at your own pleasure. Drama is action, sir, action and not confounded philosophy.

THE FATHER. All right. I'll do just as much arguing and philosophizing as everybody does when he is considering his own torments.

THE MANAGER. If the drama permits! But for Heaven's sake, man, let's get along and come to the scene.

THE STEP-DAUGHTER. It seems to me we've got too much action with our coming into his house (*indicating*

Father). You said, before, you couldn't change the scene every five minutes.

THE MANAGER. Of course not. What we've got to do is to combine and group up all the facts in one simultaneous, close-knit, action. We can't have it as you want, with your little brother wandering like a ghost from room to room, hiding behind doors and meditating a project which— what did you say it did to him?

THE STEP-DAUGHTER. Consumes him, sir, wastes him away!

THE MANAGER. Well, it may be, And then at the same time, you want the little girl there to be playing in the garden . . . one in the house, and the other in the garden: isn't that it?

THE STEP-DAUGHTER. Yes, in the sun, in the sun! That is my only pleasure: to see her happy and careless in the garden after the misery and squalor of the horrible room where we all four slept together. And I had to sleep with her—I, do you understand?—with my vile contaminated body next to hers; with her folding me fast in her loving little arms. In the garden, whenever she spied me, she would run to take me by the hand. She didn't care for the big flowers, only the little ones; and she loved to show me them and pet me.

THE MANAGER. Well then, we'll have it in the garden. Everything shall happen in the garden; and we'll group the other scenes there. (*Calls a stage hand*). Here, a backcloth with trees and something to do as a fountain basin. (*Turning round to look at the back of the stage*). Ah, you've fixed it up. Good! (*To Step-Daughter*). This is just to give an idea, of course. The Boy, instead of hiding behind the doors, will wander about here in the garden, hiding behind the trees. But it's going to be rather difficult to find a child to do that scene with you where she shows you the flowers. (*Turning to the Youth*). Come forward a little, will you please? Let's try it now! Come along! come along! (*Then seeing him come shyly forward, full of fear and looking lost*). It's a nice business, this lad here. What's the matter with him? We'll have to give him a word or two to say. (*Goes close to him, puts a hand on his shoulders, and leads him behind one of the trees*). Come on! come on! Let me see you a little! Hide here . . . yes, like that. Try and show your head just a little as if you were looking for someone . . . (*Goes back to observe the effect, when the Boy at once goes through the action*). Excellent! fine! (*Turning to Step-Daughter*). Suppose the little girl there were to surprise him as he looks round, and run over to him, so we could give him a word or two to say?

THE STEP-DAUGHTER. It's useless to hope he will speak, as long as that fellow there is here . . . (*Indicates the Son*). You must send him away first.

THE SON (*jumping up.*) Delighted! delighted! I don't ask for anything better. (*Begins to move away*).

THE MANAGER (*at once stopping him*). No! No! Where are you going? Wait a bit!

(*The Mother gets up alarmed and terrified at the thought that he is really about to go away. Instinctively she lifts her arms to prevent him, without, however, leaving her seat*).

THE SON (*to Manager who stops him*). I've got nothing to do with this affair. Let me go please! Let me go!

THE MANAGER. What do you mean by saying you've got nothing to do with this?

THE STEP-DAUGHTER (*calmly, with irony*). Don't bother to stop him: he won't go away.

THE FATHER. He has to act the terrible scene in the garden with his mother.

THE SON (*suddenly resolute and with dignity*). I shall

act nothing at all. I've said so from the very beginning (*to the Manager*). Let me go!

THE STEP-DAUGHTER (*going over to the Manager*). Allow me? (*Puts down the Manager's arm which is restraining the Son*). Well, go away then, if you want to! (*The Son looks at her with contempt and hatred. She laughs and says*). You see, he can't, he can't go away! He is obliged to stay here, indissolubly bound to the chain. If I, who fly off when that happens which has to happen, because I can't bear him—if I am still here and support that face and expression of his, you can well imagine that he is unable to move. He has to remain here, has to stop with that nice father of his, and that mother whose only son he is. (*Turning to the Mother*). Come on, mother, come along! (*Turning to Manager to indicate her*). You see, she was getting up to keep him back. (*To the Mother, beckoning her with her hand*). Come on! come on! (*Then to Manager*). You can imagine how little she wants to show these actors of yours what she really feels; but so eager is she to get near him that . . . There, you see? She is willing to act her part. (*And in fact, the Mother approaches him; and as soon as the Step-Daughter has finished speaking, opens her arms to signify that she consents*).

THE SON (*suddenly*). No! no! If I can't go away, then I'll stop here; but I repeat: I act nothing!

THE FATHER (*to Manager excitedly*). You can force him, sir.

THE SON. Nobody can force me.

THE FATHER. I can.

THE STEP-DAUGHTER. Wait a minute, wait . . . First of all, the baby has to go to the fountain . . . (*Runs to take the Child and leads her to the fountain*).

THE MANAGER. Yes, yes of course; that's it. Both at the same time.

(*The second Lady Lead and the Juvenile Lead at this point separate themselves from the group of actors. One watches the Mother attentively; the other moves about studying the movements and manner of the Son whom he will have to act*).

THE SON (*to Manager*). What do you mean by both at the same time? It isn't right. There was no scene between me and her. (*Indicates the Mother*). Ask her how it was!

THE MOTHER. Yes, it's true. I had come into his room . . .

THE SON. Into my room, do you understand? Nothing to do with the garden.

THE MANAGER. It doesn't matter. Haven't I told you we've got to group the action?

THE SON (*observing the Juvenile Lead studying him*). What do you want?

THE JUVENILE LEAD. Nothing! I was just looking at you.

THE SON (*turning towards the second Lady Lead*). Ah! she's at it too: to re-act her part (*indicating the Mother*)!

THE MANAGER. Exactly! And it seems to me that you ought to be grateful to them for their interest.

THE SON. Yes, but haven't you yet perceived that it isn't possible to live in front of a mirror which not only freezes us with the image of ourselves, but throws our likeness back at us with a horrible grimace?

THE FATHER. That is true, absolutely true. You must see that.

THE MANAGER (*to second Lady Lead and Juvenile Lead*). He's right! Move away from them!

THE SON. Do as you like. I'm out of this!

THE MANAGER. Be quiet, you, will you? And let me hear your mother! (*To Mother*). You were saying you had entered . . .

THE MOTHER. Yes, into his room, because I couldn't stand it any longer. I went to empty my heart to him of all the anguish that tortures me . . . But as soon as he saw me come in . . .

THE SON. Nothing happened! There was no scene. I went away, that's all! I don't care for scenes!

THE MOTHER. It's true, true. That's how it was.

THE MANAGER. Well now, we've got to do this bit between you and him. It's indispensable.

THE MOTHER. I'm ready . . . when you are ready. If you could only find a chance for me to tell him what I feel here in my heart.

THE FATHER (*going to Son in a great rage*). You'll do this for your mother, for your mother, do you understand?

THE SON (*quite determined*). I do nothing!

THE FATHER (*taking hold of him and shaking him*). For God's sake, do as I tell you! Don't you hear your mother asking you for a favour? Haven't you even got the guts to be a son?

THE SON (*taking hold of the Father*). No! No! And for God's sake stop it, or else . . . (*General agitation. The Mother, frightened, tries to separate them*).

THE MOTHER (*pleading*). Please! please!

THE FATHER (*not leaving hold of the Son*). You've got to obey, do you hear?

THE SON (*almost crying from rage*). What does it mean, this madness you've got? (*They separate*). Have you no decency, that you insist on showing everyone our shame? I won't do it! I won't! And I stand for the will of our author in this. He didn't want to put us on the stage, after all!

THE MANAGER. Man alive! You came here . . .

THE SON (*indicating Father*). He did! I didn't!

THE MANAGER. Aren't you here now?

THE SON. It was his wish, and he dragged us along with him. He's told you not only the things that did happen, but also things that have never happened at all.

THE MANAGER. Well, tell me then what did happen. You went out of your room without saying a word?

THE SON. Without a word, so as to avoid a scene!

THE MANAGER. And then what did you do?

THE SON. Nothing . . . walking in the garden . . . (*hesitates for a moment with expression of gloom*).

THE MANAGER (*coming closer to him, interested by his extraordinary reserve*). Well, well . . . walking in the garden . . .

THE SON (*exasperated*). Why on earth do you insist? It's horrible! (*The Mother trembles, sobs, and looks towards the fountain*).

THE MANAGER (*slowly observing the glance and turning towards the Son with increasing apprehension*). The baby?

THE SON. There in the fountain . . .

THE FATHER (*pointing with tender pity to the Mother*). She was following him at the moment . . .

THE MANAGER (*to the Son anxiously*). And then you . . .

THE SON. I ran over to her; I was jumping in to drag her out when I saw something that froze my blood . . . the boy there standing stock still, with eyes like a madman's, watching his little drowned sister, in the fountain! (*The Step-Daughter bends over the fountain to hide the Child. She sobs*). Then . . . (*A revolver shot rings out behind the trees where the Boy is hidden*).

THE MOTHER. (*With a cry of terror runs over in that direction together with several of the actors amid general confusion*).

My son! My son! (*Then amid the cries and exclamations one hears her voice*). Help! Help!

THE MANAGER (*pushing the actors aside while they lift up the Boy and carry him off*). Is he really wounded?

SOME ACTORS. He's dead! dead!

OTHER ACTORS. No, no, it's only make believe, it's only pretence!

THE FATHER (*with a terrible cry*). Pretence? Reality, sir, reality!

THE MANAGER. Pretence? Reality? To hell with it all! Never in my life has such a thing happened to me. I've lost a whole day over these people, a whole day!

Curtain.

"HENRY IV."
(Enrico Quarto)
A TRAGEDY IN THREE ACTS
BY
LUIGI PIRANDELLO
TRANSLATED BY
EDWARD STORER

CHARACTERS.

"HENRY IV." THE MARCHIONESS MATILDA SPINA. HER DAUGHTER FRIDA. THE YOUNG MARQUIS CHARLES DI NOLLI. BARON TITO BELCREDI. DOCTOR DIONYSIUS GENONI. THE FOUR PRIVATE COUNSELLORS: HAROLD (FRANK), LANDOLPH (LOLO), ORDULPH (MOMO), BERTHOLD (FINO). (*The names in brackets are nicknames*). JOHN, THE OLD WAITER. THE TWO VALETS IN COSTUME.

A SOLITARY VILLA IN ITALY IN OUR OWN TIME.

"HENRY IV."

A TRAGEDY IN THREE ACTS

ACT I

Salon in the villa, furnished and decorated so as to look exactly like the throne room of Henry IV. in the royal residence at Goslar. Among the antique decorations there are two modern life-size portraits in oil painting. They are placed against the back wall, and mounted in a wooden stand that runs the whole length of the wall. (It is wide and protrudes, so that it is like a large bench). One of the paintings is on the right; the other on the left of the throne, which is in the middle of the wall and divides the stand.

The Imperial chair and Baldachin.

The two portraits represent a lady and a gentleman, both young, dressed up in carnival costumes: one as "Henry IV.," the other as the "Marchioness Matilda of Tuscany." Exits to Right and Left.

(When the curtain goes up, the two valets jump down, as if surprised, from the stand on which they have been lying, and go and take their positions, as rigid as statues, on either side below the throne with their halberds in their hands. Soon after, from the second exit, right, enter Harold, Landolph, Ordulph and Berthold, young men employed by the Marquis Charles Di Nolli to play the part of "Secret Counsellors" at the court of "Henry IV." They are, therefore, dressed like German knights of the XIth century. Berthold,

nicknamed Fino, is just entering on his duties for the first time. His companions are telling him what he has to do and amusing themselves at his expense. The scene is to be played rapidly and vivaciously).

LANDOLPH (*to Berthold as if explaining*). And this is the throne room.

HAROLD. At Goslar.

ORDULPH. Or at the castle in the Hartz, if you prefer.

HAROLD. Or at Wurms.

LANDOLPH. According as to what's doing, it jumps about with us, now here, now there.

ORDULPH. In Saxony.

HAROLD. In Lombardy.

LANDOLPH. On the Rhine.

ONE OF THE VALETS (*without moving, just opening his lips*). I say . . .

HAROLD (*turning round*). What is it?

FIRST VALET (*like a statue*). Is he coming in or not? (*He alludes to Henry IV.*)

ORDULPH. No, no, he's asleep. You needn't worry.

SECOND VALET (*releasing his pose, taking a long breath and going to lie down again on the stand*). You might have told us at once.

FIRST VALET (*going over to Harold*). Have you got a match, please?

LANDOLPH. What? You can't smoke a pipe here, you know.

FIRST VALET (*while Harold offers him a light*). No; a cigarette. (*Lights his cigarette and lies down again on the stand*).

BERTHOLD (*who has been looking on in amazement, walking round the room, regarding the costumes of the others*). I say . . . this room . . . these costumes . . . Which Henry IV. is it? I don't quite get it. Is he Henry IV. of France or not? (*At this Landolph, Harold, and Ordulph, burst out laughing*).

LANDOLPH (*still laughing; and pointing to Berthold as if inviting the others to make fun of him*). Henry of France he says: ha! ha!

ORDULPH. He thought it was the king of France!

HAROLD. Henry IV. of Germany, my boy: the Salian dynasty!

ORDULPH. The great and tragic Emperor!

LANDOLPH. He of Canossa. Every day we carry on here the terrible war between Church and State, by Jove.

ORDULPH. The Empire against the Papacy!

HAROLD. Antipopes against the Pope!

LANDOLPH. Kings against antikings!

ORDULPH. War on the Saxons!

HAROLD. And all the rebels Princes!

LANDOLPH. Against the Emporer's own sons!

BERTHOLD (*covering his head with his hands to protect himself against this avalanche of information*). I understand! I understand! Naturally, I didn't get the idea at first. I'm right then: these aren't costumes of the XVIth century?

HAROLD. XVIth century be hanged!

ORDULPH. We're somewhere between a thousand and eleven hundred.

LANDOLPH. Work it out for yourself: if we are before Canossa on the 25th of January, 1071 . . .

BERTHOLD (*more confused than ever*). Oh my God! What a mess I've made of it!

ORDULPH. Well, just slightly, if you supposed you were at the French court.

BERTHOLD. All that historical stuff I've swatted up!

LANDOLPH. My dear boy, it's four hundred years earlier.

BERTHOLD (*getting angry*). Good Heavens! You ought

to have told me it was Germany and not France. I can't tell you how many books I've read in the last fifteen days.

HAROLD. But I say, surely you knew that poor Tito was Adalbert of Bremen, here?

BERTHOLD. Not a damned bit!

LANDOLPH. Well, don't you see how it is? When Tito died, the Marquis Di Nolli . . .

BERTHOLD. Oh, it was he, was it? He might have told me.

HAROLD. Perhaps he thought you knew.

LANDOLPH. He didn't want to engage anyone else in substitution. He thought the remaining three of us would do. But *he* began to cry out: "With Adalbert driven away . . . ": because, you see, he didn't imagine poor Tito was dead; but that, as Bishop Adalbert, the rival bishops of Cologne and Mayence had driven him off . . .

BERTHOLD (*taking his head in his hand*). But I don't know a word of what you're talking about.

ORDULPH. So much the worse for you, my boy!

HAROLD. But the trouble is that not even we know who you are.

BERTHOLD. What? Not even you? You don't know who I'm supposed to be?

ORDULPH. Hum! "Berthold."

BERTHOLD. But which Berthold? And why Berthold?

LANDOLPH (*solemnly imitating Henry IV.*). "They've driven Adalbert away from me. Well then, I want Berthold! I want Berthold!" That's what he said.

HAROLD. We three looked one another in the eyes: who's got to be Berthold?

ORDULPH. And so here you are, "Berthold," my dear fellow!

LANDOLPH. I'm afraid you will make a bit of a mess of it.

BERTHOLD (*indignant, getting ready to go*). Ah, no! Thanks very much, but I'm off! I'm out of this!

HAROLD (*restraining him with the other two, amid laughter*). Steady now! Don't get excited!

LANDOLPH. Cheer up, my dear fellow! We don't any of us know who we are really. He's Harold; he's Ordulph; I'm Landolph! That's the way he calls us. We've got used to it. But who are we? Names of the period! Yours, too, is a name of the period: Berthold! Only one of us, poor Tito, had got a really decent part, as you can read in history: that of the Bishop of Bremen. He was just like a real bishop. Tito did it awfully well, poor chap!

HAROLD. Look at the study he put into it!

LANDOLPH. Why, he even ordered his Majesty about, opposed his views, guided and counselled him. We're "secret counsellors"—in a manner of speaking only; because it is written in history that Henry IV. was hated by the upper aristocracy for surrounding himself at court with young men of the bourgeoise.

ORDULPH. Us, that is.

LANDOLPH. Yes, small devoted vassals, a bit dissolute and very gay . . .

BERTHOLD. So I've got to be gay as well?

HAROLD. I should say so! Same as we are!

ORDULPH. And it isn't too easy, you know.

LANDOLPH. It's a pity; because the way we're got up, we could do a fine historical reconstruction. There's any amount of material in the story of Henry IV. But, as a matter of fact, we do nothing. We've have the form without the content. We're worse than the real secret counsellors of Henry IV.; because certainly no one had given them a part to play—at any rate, they didn't feel they had a part to play. It was their life. They looked after their own interests at the expense of others, sold investitures and—

what not! We stop here in this magnificent court—for what?—Just doing nothing. We're like so many puppets hung on the wall, waiting for some one to come and move us or make us talk.

HAROLD. Ah no, old sport, not quite that! We've got to give the proper answer, you know. There's trouble if he asks you something and you don't chip in with the cue.

LANDOLPH. Yes, that's true.

BERTHOLD. Don't rub it in too hard! How the devil am I to give him the proper answer, if I've swatted up Henry IV. of France, and now he turns out to be Henry IV. of Germany? (*The other three laugh*).

HAROLD. You'd better start and prepare yourself at once.

ORDULPH. We'll help you out.

HAROLD. We've got any amount of books on the subject. A brief run through the main points will do to begin with.

ORDULPH. At any rate, you must have got some sort of general idea.

HAROLD. Look here! (*Turns him around and shows him the portrait of the Marchioness Matilda on the wall*). Who's that?

BERTHOLD (*looking at it*). That? Well, the thing seems to me somewhat out of place, anyway: two modern paintings in the midst of all this respectable antiquity!

HAROLD. You're right! They weren't there in the beginning. There are two niches there behind the pictures. They were going to put up two statues in the style of the period. Then the places were covered with those canvasses there.

LANDOLPH (*interrupting and continuing*). They would certainly be out of place if they really were paintings!

BERTHOLD. What are they, if they aren't paintings?

LANDOLPH. Go and touch them! Pictures all right . . .

but for him! (*Makes a mysterious gesture to the right, alluding to Henry IV.*) . . . who never touches them! . . .

BERTHOLD. No? What are they for him?

LANDOLPH. Well, I'm only supposing, you know; but I imagine I'm about right. They're images such as . . . well—such as a mirror might throw back. Do you understand? That one there represents himself, as he is in this throne room, which is all in the style of the period. What's there to marvel at? If we put you before a mirror, won't you see yourself, alive, but dressed up in ancient costume? Well, it's as if there were two mirrors there, which cast back living images in the midst of a world which, as you will see, when you have lived with us, comes to life too.

BERTHOLD. I say, look here . . . I've no particular desire to go mad here.

HAROLD. Go mad, be hanged! You'll have a fine time!

BERTHOLD. Tell me this: how have you all managed to become so learned?

LANDOLPH. My dear fellow, you can't go back over 800 years of history without picking up a bit of experience.

HAROLD. Come on! Come on! You'll see how quickly you get into it!

ORDULPH. You'll learn wisdom, too, at this school.

BERTHOLD. Well, for Heaven's sake, help me a bit! Give me the main lines, anyway.

HAROLD. Leave it to us. We'll do it all between us.

LANDOLPH. We'll put your wires on you and fix you up like a first class marionette. Come along! (*They take him by the arm to lead him away*).

BERTHOLD (*stopping and looking at the portrait on the wall*). Wait a minute! You haven't told me who that is. The Emperor's wife?

HAROLD. No! The Emperor's wife is Bertha of Susa, the sister of Amadeus II. of Savoy.

ORDULPH. And the Emperor, who wants to be young with us, can't stand her, and wants to put her away.

LANDOLPH. That is his most ferocious enemy: Matilda, Marchioness of Tuscany.

BERTHOLD. Ah, I've got it: the one who gave hospitality to the Pope!

LANDOLPH. Exactly: at Canossa!

ORDULPH. Pope Gregory VII.!

HAROLD. Our *bête noir!* Come on! come on! (*All four move toward the right to go out, when, from the left, the old servant John enters in evening dress*).

JOHN (*quickly, anxiously*). Hss! Hss! Frank! Lolo!

HAROLD (*turning round*). What is it?

BERTHOLD (*marvelling at seeing a man in modern clothes enter the throne room*). Oh! I say, this is a bit too much, this chap here!

LANDOLPH. A man of the XXth century, here! Oh, go away! (*They run over to him, pretending to menace him and throw him out*).

ORDULPH (*heroically*). Messenger of Gregory VII., away!

HAROLD. Away! Away!

JOHN (*annoyed, defending himself*). Oh, stop it! Stop it, I tell you!

ORDULPH. No, you can't set foot here!

HAROLD. Out with him!

LANDOLPH (*to Berthold*). Magic, you know! He's a demon conjured up by the Wizard of Rome! Out with your swords! (*Makes as if to draw a sword*).

JOHN (*shouting*). Stop it, will you? Don't play the fool with me! The Marquis has arrived with some friends . . .

LANDOLPH. Good! Good! Are there ladies too?

ORDULPH. Old or young?

JOHN. There are two gentlemen.
HAROLD. But the ladies, the ladies, who are they?
JOHN. The Marchioness and her daughter.
LANDOLPH (*surprised*). What do you say?
ORDULPH. The Marchioness?
JOHN. The Marchioness! The Marchioness!
HAROLD. Who are the gentlemen?
JOHN. I don't know.
HAROLD (*to Berthold*). They're coming to bring us a message from the Pope, do you see?
ORDULPH. All messengers of Gregory VII.! What fun!
JOHN. Will you let me speak, or not?
HAROLD. Go on, then!
JOHN. One of the two gentlemen is a doctor, I fancy.
LANDOLPH. Oh, I see, one of the usual doctors.
HAROLD. Bravo Berthold, you'll bring us luck!
LANDOLPH. You wait and see how we'll manage this doctor!
BERTHOLD. It looks as if I were going to get into a nice mess right away.
JOHN. If the gentlemen would allow me to speak . . . they want to come here into the throne room.
LANDOLPH (*surprised*). What? She? The Marchioness here?
HAROLD. Then this is something quite different! No play-acting this time!
LANDOLPH. We'll have a real tragedy: that's what!
BERTHOLD (*curious*). Why? Why?
ORDULPH (*pointing to the portrait*). She is that person there, don't you understand?
LANDOLPH. The daughter is the fiancée of the Marquis. But what have they come for, I should like to know?
ORDULPH. If he sees her, there'll be trouble.

LANDOLPH. Perhaps he won't recognize her any more.

JOHN. You must keep him there, if he should wake up . . .

ORDULPH. Easier said than done, by Jove!

HAROLD. You know what he's like!

JOHN. — even by force, if necessary! Those are my orders. Go on! Go on!

HAROLD. Yes, because who knows if he hasn't already wakened up?

ORDULPH. Come on then!

LANDOLPH (*going towards John with the others*). You'll tell us later what it all means.

JOHN (*shouting after them*). Close the door there, and hide the key! That other door too. (*Pointing to the other door on right*).

JOHN (*to the two valets*). Be off, you two! There (*pointing to exit right*)! Close the door after you, and hide the key!

(*The two valets go out by the first door on right. John moves over to the left to show in: Donna Matilda Spina, the young Marchioness Frida, Dr. Dionysius Genoni, the Baron Tito Belcredi and the young Marquis Charles Di Nolli, who, as master of the house, enters last.*

DONNA MATILDA SPINA *is about 45, still handsome, although there are too patent signs of her attempts to remedy the ravages of time with make-up. Her head is thus rather like a Walkyrie. This facial make-up contrasts with her beautiful sad mouth. A widow for many years, she now has as her friend the Baron Tito Belcredi, whom neither she nor anyone else takes seriously—at least so it would appear.*

What TITO BELCREDI *really is for her at bottom, he alone knows; and he is, therefore, entitled to laugh, if his friend feels the need of pretending not to know. He can always laugh at the jests which the beautiful Marchioness makes* with the others at his expense. *He is slim, prematurely gray, and younger than she is. His head is bird-like in shape. He would be a very vivacious person, if his ductile agility (which among other things makes him a redoubtable swordsman) were not enclosed in a sheath of Arab-like laziness, which is revealed in his strange, nasal drawn-out voice.*

FRIDA, *the daughter of the Marchioness is 19. She is sad; because her imperious and too beautiful mother puts her in the shade, and provokes facile gossip against her daughter as well as against herself. Fortunately for her, she is engaged to the Marquis Charles Di Nolli.*

CHARLES DI NOLLI *is a stiff young man, very indulgent towards others, but sure of himself for what he amounts to in the world. He is worried about all the responsibilities which he believes weigh on him. He is dressed in deep mourning for the recent death of his mother.*

DR. DIONYSIUS GENONI *has a bold rubicund Satyr-like face, prominent eyes, a pointed beard (which is silvery and shiny) and elegant manners. He is nearly bald. All enter in a state of perturbation, almost as if afraid, and all (except Di Nolli) looking curiously about the room. At first, they speak sotto voce.*

DI NOLLI (*to John*). Have you given the orders properly?
JOHN. Yes, my Lord; don't be anxious about that.
BELCREDI. Ah, magnificent! magnificent!
DOCTOR. How extremely interesting! Even in the surroundings his raving madness—is perfectly taken into account!
DONNA MATILDA (*glancing round for her portrait, discovers it, and goes up close to it*). Ah! Here it is! (*Going back to admire it, while mixed emotions stir within her*). Yes . . . yes . . . (*Calls her daughter Frida*).
FRIDA. Ah, your portrait!

Donna Matilda. No, no . . . look again; it's you, not I, there!

Di Nolli. Yes, it's quite true. I told you so, I . . .

Donna Matilda. But I would never have believed it! (*Shaking as if with a chill*). What a strange feeling it gives one! (*Then looking at her daughter*). Frida, what's the matter? (*She pulls her to her side, and slips an arm round her waist*). Come: don't you see yourself in me there?

Frida. Well, I really . . .

Donna Matilda. Don't you think so? Don't you, really? (*Turning to Belcredi*). Look at it, Tito! Speak up, man!

Belcredi (*without looking*). Ah, no! I shan't look at it. For me, *a priori*, certainly not!

Donna Matilda. Stupid! You think you are paying me a compliment! (*Turing to Doctor Genoni*). What do you say, Doctor? Do say something, please!

Doctor (*makes a movement to go near to the picture*).

Belcredi (*with his back turned, pretending to attract his attention secretely*). —Hss! No, doctor! For the love of Heaven, have nothing to do with it!

Doctor (*getting bewildered and smiling*). And why shouldn't I?

Donna Matilda. Don't listen to him! Come here! He's insufferable!

Frida. He acts the fool by profession, didn't you know that?

Belcredi (*to the Doctor, seeing him go over*). Look at your feet, doctor! Mind where you're going!

Doctor. Why?

Belcredi. Be careful you don't put your foot in it!

Doctor (*laughing feebly*). No, no. After all, it seems to me there's no reason to be astonished at the fact that a daughter should resemble her mother!

BELCREDI. Hullo! Hullo! He's done it now; he's said it.

DONNA MATILDA (*with exaggerated anger, advancing towards Belcredi*). What's the matter? What has he said? What has he done?

DOCTOR (*candidly*). Well, isn't it so?

BELCREDI (*answering the Marchioness*). I said there was nothing to be astounded at—and you are astounded! And why so, then, if the thing is so simple and natural for you now?

DONNA MATILDA (*still more angry*). Fool! fool! It's just because it is so natural! Just because it isn't my daughter who is there. (*Pointing to the canvass*). That is my portrait; and to find my daughter there instead of me fills me with astonishment, an astonishment which, I beg you to believe, is sincere. I forbid you to cast doubts on it.

FRIDA (*slowly and wearily*). My God! It's always like this . . . rows over nothing. . .

BELCREDI (*also slowly, looking dejected, in accents of apology*). I cast no doubt on anything! I noticed from the beginning that you haven't shared your mother's astonishment; or, if something did astonish you, it was because the likeness between you and the portrait seemed so strong.

DONNA MATILDA. Naturally! She cannot recognize herself in me as I was at her age; while I, there, can very well recognize myself in her as she is now!

DOCTOR. Quite right! Because a portrait is always there fixed in the twinkling of an eye: for the young lady something far away and without memories, while, for the Marchioness, it can bring back everything: movements, gestures, looks, smiles, a whole heap of things . . .

DONNA MATILDA. Exactly!

DOCTOR (*continuing, turning towards her*). Naturally enough, you can live all these old sensations again in your daughter.

DONNA MATILDA. He always spoils every innocent pleasure for me, every touch I have of spontaneous sentiment! He does it merely to annoy me.

DOCTOR (*frightened at the disturbance he has caused, adopts a professorial tone*). Likeness, dear Baron, is often the result of imponderable things. So one explains that . . .

BELCREDI (*interrupting the discourse*). Somebody will soon be finding a likeness between you and me, my dear professor!

DI NOLLI. Oh! let's finish with this, please! (*Points to the two doors on the Right, as a warning that there is someone there who may be listening*). We've wasted too much time as it is!

FRIDA. As one might expect when *he's* present (*alludes to Belcredi*).

DI NOLLI. Enough! The doctor is here; and we have come for a very serious purpose which you all know is important for me.

DOCTOR. Yes, that is so! But now, first of all, let's try to get some points down exactly. Excuse me, Marchioness, will you tell me why your portrait is here? Did you present it to him then?

DONNA MATILDA. No, not at all. How could I have given it to him? I was just like Frida then—and not even engaged. I gave it to him three or four years after the accident. I gave it to him because his mother wished it so much (*points to Di Nolli*) . . .

DOCTOR. She was his sister (*alludes to Henry IV.*)?

DI NOLLI. Yes, doctor; and our coming here is a debt we pay to my mother who has been dead for more than a month. Instead of being here, she and I (*indicating Frida*) ought to be traveling together . . .

DOCTOR. . . . taking a cure of quite a different kind!

Di Nolli. —Hum! Mother died in the firm conviction that her adored brother was just about to be cured.

Doctor. And can't you tell me, if you please, how she inferred this?

Di Nolli. The conviction would appear to have derived from certain strange remarks which he made, a little before mother died.

Doctor. Oh, remarks! . . . Ah! . . . It would be extremely useful for me to have those remarks, word for word, if possible.

Di Nolli. I can't remember them. I know that mother returned awfully upset from her last visit with him. On her death-bed, she made me promise that I would never neglect him, that I would have doctors see him, and examine him.

Doctor. Um! Um! Let me see! let me see! Sometimes very small reasons determine . . . and this portrait here then? . . .

Donna Matilda. For Heaven's sake, doctor, don't attach excessive importance to this. It made an impression on me because I had not seen it for so many years!

Doctor. If you please, quietly, quietly . . .

Di Nolli. —Well, yes, it must be about fifteen years ago.

Donna Matilda. More, more: eighteen!

Doctor. Forgive me, but you don't quite know what I'm trying to get at. I attach a very great importance to these two portraits . . . They were painted, naturally, prior to the famous—and most regrettable pageant, weren't they?

Donna Matilda. Of course!

Doctor. That is . . . when he was quite in his right mind—that's what I've been trying to say. Was it his suggestion that they should be painted?

DONNA MATILDA. Lots of the people who took part in the pageant had theirs done as a souvenir . . .

BELCREDI. I had mine done—as "Charles of Anjou!"

DONNA MATILDA. . . . as soon as the costumes were ready.

BELCREDI. As a matter of fact, it was proposed that the whole lot of us should be hung together in a gallery of the villa where the pageant took place. But in the end, everybody wanted to keep his own portrait.

DONNA MATILDA. And I gave him this portrait of me without very much regret . . . since his mother . . . (*indicates Di Nolli*).

DOCTOR. You don't remember if it was he who asked for it?

DONNA MATILDA. Ah, that I don't remember . . . Maybe it was his sister, wanting to help out . . .

DOCTOR. One other thing: was it his idea, this pageant?

BELCREDI (*at once*). No, no, it was mine!

DOCTOR. If you please . . .

DONNA MATILDA. Don't listen to him! It was poor Belassi's idea.

BELCREDI. Belassi! What had he got to do with it?

DONNA MATILDA. Count Belassi, who died, poor fellow, two or three months after . . .

BELCREDI. But if Belassi wasn't there when . . .

DI NOLLI. Excuse me, doctor; but is it really necessary to establish whose the original idea was?

DOCTOR. It would help me, certainly!

BELCREDI. I tell you the idea was mine! There's nothing to be proud of in it, seeing what the result's been. Look here, doctor, it was like this. One evening, in the first days of November, I was looking at an illustrated German review in the club. I was merely glancing at the pictures, because I can't read German. There was a picture of the Kaiser, at some University town where he had been a student . . . I don't remember which.

DOCTOR. Bonn, Bonn!

BELCREDI. —You are right: Bonn! He was on horseback, dressed up in one of those ancient German student guild-costumes, followed by a procession of noble students, also in costume. The picture gave me the idea. Already some one at the club had spoken of a pageant for the forthcoming carnival. So I had the notion that each of us should choose for this Tower of Babel pageant to represent some character: a king, an emperor, a prince, with his queen, empress, or lady, alongside of him—and all on horseback. The suggestion was at once accepted.

DONNA MATILDA. I had my invitation from Belassi.

BELCREDI. Well, he wasn't speaking the truth! That's all I can say, if he told you the idea was his. He wasn't even at the club the evening I made the suggestion, just as he (*meaning Henry IV.*) wasn't there either.

DOCTOR. So he chose the character of Henry IV.?

DONNA MATILDA. Because I . . . thinking of my name, and not giving the choice any importance, said I would be the Marchioness Matilda of Tuscany.

DOCTOR. I . . . don't understand the relation between the two.

DONNA MATILDA. —Neither did I, to begin with, when he said that in that case he would be at my feet like Henry IV. at Canossa. I had heard of Canossa of course; but to tell the truth, I'd forgotten most of the story; and I remember I received a curious impression when I had to get up my part, and found that I was the faithful and zealous friend of Pope Gregory VII. in deadly enmity with the Emperor of Germany. Then I understood why, since I had chosen to represent his implacable enemy, he wanted to be near me in the pageant as Henry IV.

DOCTOR. Ah, perhaps because . . .

BELCREDI. —Good Heavens, doctor, because he was then paying furious court to her (*indicates the Marchioness*)! And she, naturally . . .

DONNA MATILDA. Naturally? Not naturally at all . . .

BELCREDI (*pointing to her*). She couldn't stand him . . .

DONNA MATILDA. —No, that isn't true! I didn't dislike him. Not at all! But for me, when a man begins to want to be taken seriously, well . . .

BELCREDI (*continuing for her*). He gives you the clearest proof of his stupidity.

DONNA MATILDA. No dear; not in this case; because he was never a fool like you.

BELCREDI. Anyway, I've never asked you to take me seriously.

DONNA MATILDA. Yes, I know. But with him one couldn't joke (*changing her tone and speaking to the Doctor*). One of the many misfortunes which happen to us women, Doctor, is to see before us every now and again a pair of eyes glaring at us with a contained intense promise of eternal devotion. (*Bursts out laughing*). There is nothing quite so funny. If men could only see themselves with that eternal fidelity look in their faces! I've always thought it comic; then more even than now. But I want to make a confession—I can do so after twenty years or more. When I laughed at him then, it was partly out of fear. One might have almost believed a promise from those eyes of his. But it would have been very dangerous.

DOCTOR (*with lively interest*). Ah! ah! This is most interesting! Very dangerous, you say?

DONNA MATILDA. Yes, because he was very different from the others. And then, I am . . . well . . . what shall I say? . . . a little impatient of all that is pondered, or tedious. But I was too young then, and a woman. I had

[Act I]   "HENRY IV."   93

the bit between my teeth. It would have required more courage than I felt I possessed. So I laughed at him too—with remorse, to spite myself, indeed; since I saw that my own laugh mingled with those of all the others—the other fools—who made fun of him.

BELCREDI. My own case, more or less!

DONNA MATILDA. You make people laugh at you, my dear, with your trick of always humiliating yourself. It was quite a different affair with him. There's a vast difference. And you—you know—people laugh in your face!

BELCREDI. Well, that's better than behind one's back!

DOCTOR. Let's get to the facts. He was then already somewhat exalted, if I understand rightly.

BELCREDI. Yes, but in a curious fashion, doctor.

DOCTOR. How?

BELCREDI. Well, cold-bloodedly so to speak.

DONNA MATILDA. Not at all! It was like this, doctor! He was a bit strange, certainly; but only because he was fond of life: eccentric, there!

BELCREDI. I don't say he simulated exaltation. On the contrary, he was often genuinely exalted. But I could swear, doctor, that he saw himself at once in his own exaltation. Moreover, I'm certain it made him suffer. Sometimes he had the most comical fits of rage against himself.

DOCTOR. Yes?

DONNA MATILDA. That is true.

BELCREDI (*to Donna Matilda*). And why? (*To the doctor*). Evidently, because that immediate lucidity that comes from acting, assuming a part, at once put him out of key with his own feelings, which seemed to him not exactly false, but like something he was obliged to valorize there and then as—what shall I say—as an act of intelligence, to make up for that sincere cordial warmth he felt lacking. So he improvised, exaggerated, let himself go, so as to distract and forget himself. He appeared inconstant, fatuous, and—yes—even ridiculous, sometimes.

DOCTOR. And may we say unsociable?

BELCREDI. No, not at all. He was famous for getting up things: *tableaux vivants,* dances, theatrical performances for charity: all for the fun of the thing, of course. He was a jolly good actor, you know!

DI NOLLI. Madness has made a superb actor of him.

BELCREDI. —Why, so he was even in the old days. When the accident happened, after the horse fell . . .

DOCTOR. Hit the back of his head, didn't he?

DONNA MATILDA. Oh, it was horrible! He was beside me! I saw him between the horse's hoofs! It was rearing!

BELCREDI. None of us thought it was anything serious at first. There was a stop in the pageant, a bit of disorder. People wanted to know what had happened. But they'd already taken him off to the villa.

DONNA MATILDA. There wasn't the least sign of a wound, not a drop of blood.

BELCREDI. We thought he had merely fainted.

DONNA MATILDA. But two hours afterwards . . .

BELCREDI. He reappeared in the drawing-room of the villa . . . that is what I wanted to say . . .

DONNA MATILDA. My God! What a face he had. I saw the whole thing at once!

BELCREDI. No, no! that isn't true. Nobody saw it, doctor, believe me!

DONNA MATILDA. Doubtless, because you were all like mad folk.

BELCREDI. Everybody was pretending to act his part for a joke. It was a regular Babel.

DONNA MATILDA. And you can imagine, doctor, what terror struck into us when we understood that he, on the contrary, was playing his part in deadly earnest . . .

DOCTOR. Oh, he was there too, was he?

BELCREDI. Of course! He came straight into the midst of us. We thought he'd quite recovered, and was pretending, fooling, like all the rest of us . . .only doing it rather better; because, as I say, he knew how to act.

DONNA MATILDA. Some of them began to hit him with their whips and fans and sticks.

BELCREDI. And then—as a king, he was armed, of course —he drew out his sword and menaced two or three of us . . . It was a terrible moment, I can assure you!

DONNA MATILDA. I shall never forget that scene—all our masked faces hideous and terrified gazing at him, at that terrible mask of his face, which was no longer a mask, but madness, madness personified.

BELCREDI. He was Henry IV., Henry IV. in person, in a moment of fury.

DONNA MATILDA. He'd got into it all the detail and minute preparation of a month's careful study. And it all burned and blazed there in the terrible obsession which lit his face.

DOCTOR. Yes, that is quite natural, of course. The momentary obsession of a dilettante became fixed, owing to the fall and the damage to the brain.

BELCREDI (*to Frida and Di Nolli*). You see the kind of jokes life can play on us. (*To Di Nolli*): You were four or five years old. (*To Frida*): Your mother imagines you've taken her place there in that portrait; when, at the time, she had not the remotest idea that she would bring you into the world. My hair is already grey; and he—look at him— (*points to portrait*)—ha! A smack on the head, and he never moves again: Henry IV. for ever!

DOCTOR (*seeking to draw the attention of the others, looking learned and imposing*). —Well, well, then it comes, we may say, to this . . .

(*Suddenly the first exit to right, the one nearest footlights, opens, and Berthold enters all excited*).

BERTHOLD (*rushing in*). I say! I say! (*Stops for a moment, arrested by the astonishment which his appearance has caused in the others*).

FRIDA (*running away terrified*). Oh dear! oh dear! it's he, it's . . .

DONNA MATILDA (*covering her face with her hands so as not to see*). Is it, is it he?

DI NOLLI. No, no, what are you talking about? Be calm!

DOCTOR. Who is it then?

BELCREDI. One of our masqueraders.

DI NOLLI. He is one of the four youths we keep here to help him out in his madness . . .

BERTHOLD. I beg your pardon, Marquis . . .

DI NOLLI. Pardon be damned! I gave orders that the doors were to be closed, and that nobody should be allowed to enter.

BERTHOLD. Yes, sir, but I can't stand it any longer, and I ask you to let me go away this very minute.

DI NOLLI. Oh, you're the new valet, are you? You were supposed to begin this morning, weren't you?

BERTHOLD. Yes, sir, and I can't stand it, I can't bear it.

DONNA MATILDA (*to Di Nolli excitedly*). What? Then he's not so calm as you said?

BERTHOLD (*quickly*). —No, no, my lady, it isn't he; it's my companions. You say "help him out with his madness," Marquis; but they don't do anything of the kind. They're the real madmen. I come here for the first time, and instead of helping me . . .

(*Landolph and Harold come in from the same door, but hesitate on the threshold*).

LANDOLPH. Excuse me?

HAROLD. May I come in, my Lord?

DI NOLLI. Come in! What's the matter? What are you all doing?

FRIDA. Oh God! I'm frightened! I'm going to run away. (*Makes towards exit at Left*).

DI NOLLI (*restraining her at once*). No, no, Frida!

LANDOLPH. My Lord, this fool here . . . (*indicates Berthold*).

BERTHOLD (*protesting*). Ah, no thanks, my friends, no thanks! I'm not stopping here! I'm off!

LANDOLPH. What do you mean — you're not stopping here?

HAROLD. He's ruined everything, my Lord, running away in here!

LANDOLPH. He's made him quite mad. We can't keep him in there any longer. He's given orders that he's to be arrested; and he wants to "judge" him at once from the throne: What is to be done?

DI NOLLI. Shut the door, man! Shut the door! Go and close that door! (*Landolph goes over to close it*).

HAROLD. Ordulph, alone, won't be able to keep him there.

LANDOLPH. —My Lord, perhaps if we could announce the visitors at once, it would turn his thoughts. Have the gentlemen thought under what pretext they will present themselves to him?

DI NOLLI. —It's all been arranged! (*To the Doctor*): If you, doctor, think it well to see him at once. . . .

FRIDA. I'm not coming! I'm not coming! I'll keep out of this. You too, mother, for Heaven's sake, come away with me!

DOCTOR. —I say . . . I suppose he's not armed, is he?

DI NOLLI. —Nonsense! Of course not. (*To Frida*):

Frida, you know this is childish of you. You wanted to come!

FRIDA. I didn't at all. It was mother's idea.

DONNA MATILDA. And I'm quite ready to see him. What are we going to do?

BELCREDI. Must we absolutely dress up in some fashion or other?

LANDOLPH. —Absolutely essential, indispensable, sir. Alas! as you see . . . (*shows his costume*), there'd be awful trouble if he saw you gentlemen in modern dress.

HAROLD. He would think it was some diabolical masquerade.

DI NOLLI. As these men seem to be in costume to you, so we appear to be in costume to him, in these modern clothes of ours.

LANDOLPH. It wouldn't matter so much if he wouldn't suppose it to be the work of his mortal enemy.

BELCREDI. Pope Gregory VII.?

LANDOLPH. Precisely. He calls him "a pagan."

BELCREDI. The Pope a pagan? Not bad that!

LANDOLPH. —Yes, sir,—and a man who calls up the dead! He accuses him of all the diabolical arts. He's terribly afraid of him.

DOCTOR. Persecution mania!

HAROLD. He'd be simply furious.

DI NOLLI (*to Belcredi*). But there's no need for you to be there, you know. It's sufficient for the doctor to see him.

DOCTOR. —What do you mean? . . . I? Alone?

DI NOLLI. —But they are there (*indicates the three young men*).

DOCTOR. I don't mean that . . . I mean if the Marchioness . . .

DONNA MATILDA. Of course. I mean to see him too, naturally. I want to see him again.

Frida. Oh, why, mother, why? Do come away with me, I implore you!

Donna Matilda (*imperiously*). Let me do as I wish! I came here for this purpose! (*To Landolph*): I shall be "Adelaide," the mother.

Landolph. Excellent! The mother of the Empress Bertha. Good! It will be enough if her Ladyship wears the ducal crown and puts on a mantle that will hide her other clothes entirely. (*To Harold*): Off you go, Harold!

Harold. Wait a moment! And this gentleman here (*alludes to the Doctor*)? . . .

Doctor. —Ah yes . . . we decided I was to be . . . the Bishop of Cluny, Hugh of Cluny!

Harold. The gentleman means the Abbot. Very good! Hugh of Cluny.

Landolph. —He's often been here before!

Doctor (*amazed*). —What? Been here before?

Landolph. —Don't be alarmed! I mean that it's an easily prepared disguise . . .

Harold. We've made use of it on other occasions, you see!

Doctor. But . . .

Landolph. Oh no, there's no risk of his remembering. He pays more attention to the dress than to the person.

Donna Matilda. That's fortunate for me too then.

Di Nolli. Frida, you and I'll get along. Come on Tito!

Belcredi. Ah no. If she (*indicates the Marchioness*) stops here, so do I!

Donna Matilda. But I don't need you at all.

Belcredi. You may not need me, but I should like to see him again myself. Mayn't I?

Landolph. Well, perhaps it would be better if there were three.

HAROLD. How is the gentleman to be dressed then?
BELCREDI. Oh, try and find some easy costume for me.
LANDOLPH (*to Harold*). Hum! Yes . . . he'd better be from Cluny too.
BELCREDI. What do you mean—from Cluny?
LANDOLPH. A Benedictine's habit of the Abbey of Cluny. He can be in attendance on Monsignor. (*To Harold*): Off you go! (*To Berthold*). And you too get away and keep out of sight all today. No, wait a bit! (*To Berthold*): You bring here the costumes he will give you. (*To Harold*): You go at once and announce the visit of the "Duchess Adelaide" and "Monsignor Hugh of Cluny." Do you understand? (*Harold and Berthold go off by the first door on the Right*).
DI NOLLI. We'll retire now. (*Goes off with Frida, left*).
DOCTOR. Shall I be a *persona grata* to him, as Hugh of Cluny?
LANDOLPH. Oh, rather! Don't worry about that! Monsignor has always been received here with great respect. You too, my Lady, he will be glad to see. He never forgets that it was owing to the intercession of you two that he was admitted to the Castle of Canossa and the presence of Gregory VII., who didn't want to receive him.
BELCREDI. And what do I do?
LANDOLPH. You stand a little apart, respectfully: that's all.
DONNA MATILDA (*irritated, nervous*). You would do well to go away, you know.
BELCREDI (*slowly, spitefully*). How upset you seem! . . .
DONNA MATILDA (*proudly*). I am as I am. Leave me alone!

(*Berthold comes in with the costumes*).

LANDOLPH (*seeing him enter*). Ah, the costumes: here they are. This mantle is for the Marchioness . . .

DONNA MATILDA. Wait a minute! I'll take off my hat. (*Does so and gives it to Berthold*).

LANDOLPH. Put it down there! (*Then to the Marchioness, while he offers to put the ducal crown on her head*). Allow me!

DONNA MATILDA. Dear, dear! Isn't there a mirror here?

LANDOLPH. Yes, there's one there (*points to the door on the Left*). If the Marchioness would rather put it on herself . . .

DONNA MATILDA. Yes, yes, that will be better. Give it to me! (*Takes up her hat and goes off with Berthold, who carries the cloak and the crown*).

BELCREDI. Well, I must say, I never thought I should be a Benedictine monk! By the way, this business must cost an awful lot of money.

THE DOCTOR. Like any other fantasy, naturally!

BELCREDI. Well, there's a fortune to go upon.

LANDOLPH. We have got there a whole wardrobe of costumes of the period, copied to perfection from old models. This is my special job. I get them from the best theatrical costumers. They cost lots of money. (*Donna Matilda re-enters, wearing mantle and crown*).

BELCREDI (*at once, in admiration*). Oh magnificent! Oh, truly regal!

DONNA MATILDA (*looking at Belcredi and bursting out into laughter*). Oh no, no! Take it off! You're impossible. You look like an ostrich dressed up as a monk.

BELCREDI. Well, how about the doctor?

THE DOCTOR. I don't think I look so bad, do I?

DONNA MATILDA. No; the doctor's all right . . . but you are too funny for words.

THE DOCTOR. Do you have many receptions here then?

LANDOLPH. It depends. He often gives orders that such and such a person appear before him. Then we have to find someone who will take the part. Women too . . .

DONNA MATILDA (*hurt, but trying to hide the fact*). Ah, women too?

LANDOLPH. Oh, yes; many at first.

BELCREDI (*laughing*). Oh, that's great! In costume, like the Marchioness?

LANDOLPH. Oh well, you know, women of the kind that lend themselves to . . .

BELCREDI. Ah, I see! (*Perfidiously to the Marchioness*): Look out, you know he's becoming dangerous for you.

(*The second door on the right opens, and Harold appears, making first of all a discreet sign that all conversation should cease*).

HAROLD. His Majesty, the Emperor!

(*The two valets enter first, and go and stand on either side of the throne. Then Henry IV. comes in between Ordulph and Harold, who keep a little in the rear respectfully.*

HENRY IV. *is about 50 and very pale. The hair on the back of his head is already grey; over the temples and forehead it appears blond, owing to its having been tinted in an evident and puerile fashion. On his cheek bones he has two small, doll-like dabs of colour, that stand out prominently against the rest of his tragic pallor. He is wearing a penitent's sack over his regal habit, as at Canossa. His eyes have a fixed look which is dreadful to see, and this expression is in strained contrast with the sackcloth. Ordulph carries the Imperial crown; Harold, the sceptre with the eagle, and the globe with the cross*).

HENRY IV. (*bowing first to Donna Matilda and afterwards to the doctor*). My lady . . . Monsignor . . .

(*Then he looks at Belcredi and seems about to greet him too; when, suddenly, he turns to Landolph, who has approached him, and asks him sotto voce and with diffidence*): Is that Peter Damiani?

LANDOLPH. No, Sire. He is a monk from Cluny who is accompanying the Abbot.

HENRY IV. (*looks again at Belcredi with increasing mistrust, and then noticing that he appears embarrassed and keeps glancing at Donna Matilda and the doctor, stands upright and cries out*). No, it's Peter Damiani! It's no use, father, your looking at the Duchess. (*Then turning quickly to Donna Matilda and the doctor as though to ward off a danger*): I swear it! I swear that my heart is changed towards your daughter. I confess that if he (*indicates Belcredi*) hadn't come to forbid it in the name of Pope Alexander, I'd have repudiated her. Yes, yes, there were people ready to favour the repudiation: the Bishop of Mayence would have done it for a matter of one hundred and twenty farms. (*Looks at Landolph a little perplexed and adds*): But I mustn't speak ill of the bishops at this moment! (*More humbly to Belcredi*): I am grateful to you, believe me, I am grateful to you for the hindrance you put in my way!—God knows, my life's been all made of humiliations: my mother, Adalbert, Tribur, Goslar! And now this sackcloth you see me wearing! (*Changes tone suddenly and speaks like one who goes over his part in a parenthesis of astuteness*). It doesn't matter: clarity of ideas, perspicacity, firmness and patience under adversity that's the thing. (*Then turning to all and speaking solemnly*). I know how to make amend for the mistakes I have made; and I can humiliate myself even before you, Peter Damiani. (*Bows profoundly to him and remains curved. Then a suspicion is born in him which he is obliged to utter in menacing tones, almost against his will*). Was it not perhaps you who started that obscene rumour that my holy mother had illicit relations with the Bishop of Augusta?

BELCREDI (*since Henry IV. has his finger pointed at him*). No, no, it wasn't I . . .

HENRY IV. (*straightening up*). Not true, not true? Infamy! (*Looks at him and then adds*): I didn't think you capable of it! (*Goes to the doctor and plucks his sleeve, while winking at him knowingly*): Always the same, Monsignor, those bishops, always the same!

HAROLD (*softly, whispering as if to help out the doctor*). Yes, yes, the rapacious bishops!

THE DOCTOR (*to Harold, trying to keep it up*). Ah, yes, those fellows . . . ah yes . . .

HENRY IV. Nothing satisfies them! I was a little boy, Monsignor . . . One passes the time, playing even, when, without knowing it, one is a king.—I was six years old; and they tore me away from my mother, and made use of me against her without my knowing anything about it . . . always profaning, always stealing, stealing! . . . One greedier than the other . . . Hanno worse than Stephen! Stephen worse than Hanno!

LANDOLPH (*sotto voce, persuasively, to call his attention*). Majesty!

HENRY IV. (*turning round quickly*). Ah yes . . . this isn't the moment to speak ill of the bishops. But this infamy against my mother, Monsignor, is too much. (*Looks at the Marchioness and grows tender*). And I can't even weep for her, Lady . . . I appeal to you who have a mother's heart! She came here to see me from her convent a month ago . . . They had told me she was dead! (*Sustained pause full of feeling. Then smiling sadly*): I can't weep for her; because if you are here now, and I am like this (*shows the sackcloth he is wearing*), it means I am twenty-six years old!

HAROLD. And that she is therefore alive, Majesty! . . .
ORDULPH. Still in her convent!
HENRY IV. (*looking at them*). Ah yes! And I can postpone my grief to another time. (*Shows the Marchioness almost with coquetery the tint he has given to his hair*). Look! I am still fair . . . (*Then slowly as if in confidence*). For you . . . there's no need! But little exterior details do help! A matter of time, Monsignor, do you understand me? (*Turns to the Marchioness and notices her hair*). Ah, but I see that you too, Duchess . . . Italian, eh (*as much as to say "false"; but without any indignation, indeed rather with malicious admiration*)? Heaven forbid that I should show disgust or surprise! Nobody cares to recognize that obscure and fatal power which sets limits to our will. But I say, if one is born and one dies . . . Did you want to be born, Monsignor? I didn't! And in both cases, independently of our wills, so many things happen we would wish didn't happen, and to which we resign ourselves as best we can! . . .
DOCTOR (*merely to make a remark, while studying Henry IV. carefully*). Alas! Yes, alas!
HENRY IV. It's like this: When we are not resigned, out come our desires. A woman wants to be a man . . . an old man would be young again. Desires, ridiculous fixed ideas of course—But reflect! Monsignor, those other desires are not less ridiculous: I mean, those desires where the will is kept within the limits of the possible. Not one of us can lie or pretend. We're all fixed in good faith in a certain concept of ourselves. However, Monsignor, while you keep yourself in order, holding on with both your hands to your holy habit, there slips down from your sleeves, there peels off from you like . . . like a serpent . . . something you don't notice: life, Monsignor! (*Turns to the Marchioness*): Has it never happened to you, my Lady, to find a different

self in yourself? Have you always been the same? My God! One day . . . how was it, how was it you were able to commit this or that action? (*Fixes her so intently in the eyes as to almost make her blanch*) : Yes, that particular action, that very one: we understand each other! But don't be afraid: I shall reveal it to none. And you, Peter Damiani, how could you be a friend of that man? . . .

LANDOLPH. Majesty!

HENRY IV. (*at once*). No, I won't name him! (*Turning to Belcredi*): What did you think of him? But we all of us cling tight to our conceptions of ourselves, just as he who is growing old dyes his hair. What does it matter that this dyed hair of mine isn't a reality for you, if it *is,* to some extent, for me?—you, you, my Lady, certainly don't dye your hair to deceive the others, nor even yourself; but only to cheat your own image a little before the looking-glass. I do it for a joke! You do it seriously! But I assure you that you too, Madam, are in masquerade, though it be in all seriousness; and I am not speaking of the venerable crown on your brows or the ducal mantle. I am speaking only of the memory you wish to fix in yourself of your fair complexion one day when it pleased you—or of your dark complexion, if you were dark: the fading image of your youth! For you, Peter Damiani, on the contrary, the memory of what you have been, of what you have done, seems to you a recognition of past realities that remain within you like a dream. I'm in the same case too: with so many inexplicable memories—like dreams! Ah! . . . There's nothing to marvel at in it, Peter Damiani! Tomorrow it will be the same thing with our life of today! (*Suddenly getting excited and taking hold of his sackcloth*). This sackcloth here . . . (*Beginning to take it off with a gesture of almost ferocious joy while the three valets run over to him, frightened, as if to prevent his doing so*)! Ah, my God! (*Draws back and throws off sackcloth*). Tomorrow, at Bressanone, twenty-seven German and Lombard bishops will sign with me the act of deposition of Gregory VII.! No Pope at all! Just a false monk!

ORDULPH (*with the other three*). Majesty! Majesty! In God's name! . . .

HAROLD (*inviting him to put on the sackcloth again*). Listen to what he says, Majesty!

LANDOLPH. Monsignor is here with the Duchess to intercede in your favor. (*Makes secret signs to the Doctor to say something at once*).

DOCTOR (*foolishly*). Ah yes . . . yes . . . we are here to intercede . . .

HENRY IV. (*repeating at once, almost terrified, allowing the three to put on the sackcloth again, and pulling it down over him with his own hands*). Pardon . . . yes . . . yes . . . pardon, Monsignor: forgive me, my Lady . . . I swear to you I feel the whole weight of the anathema. (*Bends himself, takes his face between his hands, as though waiting for something to crush him. Then changing tone, but without moving, says softly to Landolph, Harold and Ordulph*): But I don't know why I cannot be humble before that man there! (*indicates Belcredi*).

LANDOLPH (*sottovoce*). But why, Majesty, do you insist on believing he is Peter Damiani, when he isn't, at all?

HENRY IV. (*looking at him timorously*). He isn't Peter Damiani?

HAROLD. No, no, he is a poor monk, Majesty.

HENRY IV. (*sadly with a touch of exasperation*). Ah! None of us can estimate what we do when we do it from instinct . . . You perhaps, Madam, can understand me better than the others, since you are a woman and a Duchess. This is a solemn and decisive moment. I could, you know, accept the assistance of the Lombard bishops, arrest the Pope, lock him up here in the castle, run to Rome and elect an anti-Pope; offer alliance to Robert Guiscard—and Gregory VII. would be lost! I resist the temptation; and, believe me, I am wise in doing so. I feel the atmosphere of our times and the majesty of one who knows how to be what he ought to be! a Pope! Do you feel inclined to laugh at me, seeing me like this? You would be foolish to do so; for you don't understand the political wisdom which makes this penitent's sack advisable. The parts may be changed tomorrow. What would you do then? Would you laugh to see the Pope a prisoner? No! It would come to the same thing: I dressed as a penitent, today; he, as prisoner tomorrow! But woe to him who doesn't know how to wear his mask, be he king or Pope!—Perhaps he is a bit too cruel! No! Yes, yes, maybe!—You remember, my Lady, how your daughter Bertha, for whom, I repeat, my feelings have changed (*turns to Belcredi and shouts to his face as if he were being contradicted by him*)—yes, changed on account of the affection and devotion she showed me in that terrible moment . . . (*then once again to the Marchioness*) . . . you remember how she came with me, my Lady, followed me like a beggar and passed two nights out in the open, in the snow? You are her mother! Doesn't this touch your mother's heart? Doesn't this urge you to pity, so that you will beg His Holiness for pardon, beg him to receive us?

DONNA MATILDA (*trembling, with feeble voice*). Yes, yes, at once . . .

DOCTOR. It shall be done!

HENRY IV. And one thing more! (*Draws them in to listen to him*). It isn't enough that he should receive me! You know he can do *everything*—*everything* I tell you! He can even call up the dead. (*Touches his chest*): Behold me! Do you see me? There is no magic art unknown to him. Well, Monsignor, my Lady, my torment is really this:

that whether here or there (*pointing to his portrait almost in fear*) I can't free myself from this magic. I am a penitent now, you see; and I swear to you I shall remain so until he receives me. But you two, when the excommunication is taken off, must ask the Pope to do this thing he can so easily do: to take me away from that (*indicating the portrait again*); and let me live wholly and freely my miserable life. A man can't always be twenty-six, my Lady. I ask this of you for your daughter's sake too; that I may love her as she deserves to be loved, well disposed as I am now, all tender towards her for her pity. There: it's all there! I am in your hands! (*Bows*). My Lady! Monsignor!

(*He goes off, bowing grandly, through the door by which he entered, leaving everyone stupefied, and the Marchioness so profoundly touched, that no sooner has he gone than she breaks out into sobs and sits down almost fainting*).

ACT II

(*Another room of the villa, adjoining the throne room. Its furniture is antique and severe. Principal exit at rear in the background. To the left, two windows looking on the garden. To the right, a door opening into the throne room.*
  Late afternoon of the same day.
  Donna Matilda, the doctor and Belcredi are on the stage engaged in conversation; but Donna Matilda stands to one side, evidently annoyed at what the other two are saying; although she cannot help listening, because, in her agitated state, everything interests her in spite of herself. The talk of the other two attracts her attention, because she instinctively feels the need for calm at the moment).

BELCREDI. It may be as you say, doctor, but that was my impression.
  DOCTOR. I won't contradict you; but, believe me, it is only . . . an impression.
  BELCREDI. Pardon me, but he even said so, and quite clearly (*turning to the Marchioness*). Didn't he, Marchioness?
  DONNA MATILDA (*turning round*). What did he say? . . . (*Then not agreeing*). Oh yes . . . but not for the reason you think!
  DOCTOR. He was alluding to the costumes we had slipped on . . . Your cloak (*indicating the Marchioness*), our Benedictine habits . . . But all this is childish!
  DONNA MATILDA (*turning quickly, indignant*). Childish? What do you mean, doctor?

DOCTOR. From one point of view, it is—I beg you to let me say so, Marchioness! Yet, on the other hand, it is much more complicated than you can imagine.

DONNA MATILDA. To me, on the contrary, it is perfectly clear!

DOCTOR (*with a smile of pity of the competent person towards those who do not understand*). We must take into account the peculiar psychology of madmen; which, you must know, enables us to be certain that they observe things and can, for instance, easily detect people who are disguised; can in fact recognize the disguise and yet believe in it; just as children do, for whom disguise is both play and reality. That is why I used the word childish. But the thing is extremely complicated, inasmuch as he must be perfectly aware of being an image to himself and for himself—that image there, in fact (*alluding to the portrait in the throne room, and pointing to the left*)!

BELCREDI. That's what he said!

DOCTOR. Very well then—An image before which other images, ours, have appeared: understand? Now he, in his acute and perfectly lucid delirium, was able to detect at once a difference between his image and ours: that is, he saw that ours were make-believes. So he suspected us; because all madmen are armed with a special diffidence. But that's all there is to it! Our make-believe, built up all round his, did not seem pitiful to him. While his seemed all the more tragic to us, in that he, as if in defiance—understand?—and induced by his suspicion, wanted to show us up merely as a joke. That was also partly the case with him, in coming before us with painted cheeks and hair, and saying he had done it on purpose for a jest.

DONNA MATILDA (*impatiently*). No, it's not that, doctor. It's not like that! It's not like that!

DOCTOR. Why isn't it, may I ask?

DONNA MATILDA (*with decision but trembling*). I am perfectly certain he recognized me!

DOCTOR. It's not possible . . . it's not possible!

BELCREDI (*at the same time*). Of course not!

DONNA MATILDA (*more than ever determined, almost convulsively*). I tell you, he recognized me! When he came close up to speak to me—looking in my eyes, right into my eyes—he recognized me!

BELCREDI. But he was talking of your daughter!

DONNA MATILDA. That's not true! He was talking of me! Of me!

BELCREDI. Yes, perhaps, when he said . . .

DONNA MATILDA (*letting herself go*). About my dyed hair! But didn't you notice that he added at once: "or the memory of your dark hair, if you were dark"? He remembered perfectly well that I was dark—then!

BELCREDI. Nonsense! nonsense!

DONNA MATILDA (*not listening to him, turning to the doctor*). My hair, doctor, is really dark—like my daughter's! That's why he spoke of her.

BELCREDI. But he doesn't even know your daughter! He's never seen her!

DONNA MATILDA. Exactly! Oh, you never understand anything! By my daughter, stupid, he meant me—as I was then!

BELCREDI. Oh, this is catching! This is catching, this madness!

DONNA MATILDA (*softly, with contempt*). Fool!

BELCREDI. Excuse me, were you ever his wife? Your daughter is his wife—in his delirium: Bertha of Susa.

DONNA MATILDA. Exactly! Because I, no longer dark —as he remembered me—but *fair*, introduced myself as "Adelaide," the mother. My daughter doesn't exist for him:

he's never seen her—you said so yourself! So how can he know whether she's fair or dark?

BELCREDI. But he said dark, speaking generally, just as anyone who wants to recall, whether fair or dark, a memory of youth in the color of the hair! And you, as usual, begin to imagine things! Doctor, you said I ought not to have come! It's she who ought not to have come!

DONNA MATILDA (*upset for a moment by Belcredi's remark, recovers herself. Then with a touch of anger, because doubtful*). No, no . . . he spoke of me . . . He spoke all the time to me, with me, of me . . .

BELCREDI. That's not bad! He didn't leave me a moment's breathing space; and you say he was talking all the time to you? Unless you think he was alluding to you too, when he was talking to Peter Damiani!

DONNA MATILDA (*defiantly, almost exceeding the limits of courteous discussion*). Who knows? Can you tell me why, from the outset, he showed a strong dislike for you, for you alone? (*From the tone of the question, the expected answer must almost explicitly be: "because he understands you are my lover." Belcredi feels this so well that he remains silent and can say nothing*).

DOCTOR. The reason may also be found in the fact that only the visit of the Duchess Adelaide and the abbot of Cluny was announced to him. Finding a third person present, who had not been announced, at once his suspicions . . .

BELCREDI. Yes, exactly! His suspicion made him see an enemy in me: Peter Damiani! But she's got it into her head, that he recognized her . . .

DONNA MATILDA. There's no doubt about it! I could see it from his eyes, doctor. You know, there's a way of looking that leaves no doubt whatever . . . Perhaps it was only for an instant, but I am sure!

DOCTOR. It is not impossible: a lucid moment . . .

DONNA MATILDA. Yes, perhaps . . . And then his speech seemed to me full of regret for his and my youth— for the horrible thing that happened to him, that has held him in that disguise from which he has never been able to free himself, and from which he longs to be free—he said so himself!

BELCREDI. Yes, so as to be able to make love to your daughter, or you, as you believe—having been touched by your pity.

DONNA MATILDA. Which is very great, I would ask you to believe.

BELCREDI. As one can see, Marchioness; so much so that a miracle-worker might expect a miracle from it!

DOCTOR. Will you let me speak? I don't work miracles, because I am a doctor and not a miracle-worker. I listened very intently to all he said; and I repeat that that certain analogical elasticity, common to all symptomatised delirium, is evidently with him much . . . what shall I say?—much relaxed! The elements, that is, of his delirium no longer hold together. It seems to me he has lost the equilibrium of his second personality and sudden recollections drag him —and this is very comforting—not from a state of incipient apathy, but rather from a morbid inclination to reflective melancholy, which shows a . . . a very considerable cerebral activity. Very comforting, I repeat! Now if, by this violent trick we've planned . . .

DONNA MATILDA (*turning to the window, in the tone of a sick person complaining*). But how is it that the motor has not returned? It's three hours and a half since . . .

DOCTOR. What do you say?

DONNA MATILDA. The motor, doctor! It's more than three hours and a half . . .

DOCTOR (*taking out his watch and looking at it*). Yes, more than four hours, by this!

DONNA MATILDA. It could have reached here an hour ago at least! But, as usual . . .

BELCREDI. Perhaps they can't find the dress . . .

DONNA MATILDA. But I explained exactly where it was! (*impatiently*). And Frida . . . where is Frida?

BELCREDI (*looking out of the window*). Perhaps she is in the garden with Charles . . .

DOCTOR. He'll talk her out of her fright.

BELCREDI. She's not afraid, doctor; don't you believe it: the thing bores her rather . . .

DONNA MATILDA. Just don't ask anything of her! I know what she's like.

DOCTOR. Let's wait patiently. Anyhow, it will soon be over, and it has to be in the evening . . . It will only be the matter of a moment! If we can succeed in rousing him, as I was saying, and in breaking at one go the threads—already slack—which still bind him to this fiction of his, giving him back what he himself asks for—you remember, he said: "one cannot always be twenty-six years old, madam!" if we can give him freedom from this torment, which even *he* feels is a torment, then if he is able to recover at one bound the sensation of the distance of time . . .

BELCREDI (*quickly*). He'll be cured! (*then emphatically with irony*). We'll pull him out of it all!

DOCTOR. Yes, we may hope to set him going again, like a watch which has stopped at a certain hour . . . just as if we had our watches in our hands and were waiting for that other watch to go again.—A shake—so—and let's hope it'll tell the time again after its long stop. (*At this point the Marquis Charles Di Nolli enters from the principal entrance*).

DONNA MATILDA. Oh, Charles! ... And Frida? Where is she?

DI NOLLI. She'll be here in a moment.

DOCTOR. Has the motor arrived?

DI NOLLI. Yes.

DONNA MATILDA. Yes? Has the dress come?

DI NOLLI. It's been here some time.

DOCTOR. Good! Good!

DONNA MATILDA (*trembling*). Where is she? Where's Frida?

DI NOLLI (*shrugging his shoulders and smiling sadly, like one lending himself unwillingly to an untimely joke*). You'll see, you'll see! ... (*pointing towards the hall*). Here she is! ... (*Berthold appears at the threshold of the hall, and announces with solemnity*).

BERTHOLD. Her Highness the Countess Matilda of Canossa! (*Frida enters, magnificent and beautiful, arrayed in the robes of her mother as "Countess Matilda of Tuscany," so that she is a living copy of the portrait in the throne room*).

FRIDA (*passing Berthold, who is bowing, says to him with disdain*). Of Tuscany, of Tuscany! Canossa is just one of my castles!

BELCREDI (*in admiration*). Look! Look! She seems another person ...

DONNA MATILDA. One would say it were I! Look!— Why, Frida, look! She's exactly my portrait, alive!

DOCTOR. Yes, yes ... Perfect! Perfect! The portrait, to the life.

BELCREDI. Yes, there's no question about it. She *is* the portrait! Magnificent!

FRIDA. Don't make me laugh, or I shall burst! I say, mother, what a tiny waist you had? I had to squeeze so to get into this!

[ACT II]   *"HENRY IV."*   117

DONNA MATILDA (*arranging her dress a little*). Wait! . . . Keep still! . . . These pleats . . . is it really so tight?

FRIDA. I'm suffocating! I implore you, to be quick! . . .

DOCTOR. But we must wait till it's evening!

FRIDA. No, no, I can't hold out till evening!

DONNA MATILDA. Why did you put it on so soon?

FRIDA. The moment I saw it, the temptation was irresistible . . .

DONNA MATILDA. At least you could have called me, or have had someone help you! It's still all crumpled.

FRIDA. So I saw, mother; but they are old creases; they won't come out.

DOCTOR. It doesn't matter, Marchioness! The illusion is perfect. (*Then coming nearer and asking her to come in front of her daughter, without hiding her*). If you please, stay there, there . . . at a certain distance . . . now a little more forward . . .

BELCREDI. For the feeling of the distance of time . . .

DONNA MATILDA (*slightly turning to him*). Twenty years after! A disaster! A tragedy!

BELCREDI. Now don't let's exaggerate!

DOCTOR (*embarrassed, trying to save the situation*). No, no! I meant the dress . . . so as to see . . . You know . . .

BELCREDI (*laughing*). Oh, as for the dress, doctor, it isn't a matter of twenty years! It's eight hundred! An abyss! Do you really want to shove him across it (*pointing first to Frida and then to Marchioness*) from there to here? But you'll have to pick him up in pieces with a basket! Just think now: for us it is a matter of twenty years, a couple of dresses, and a masquerade. But, if, as you say, doctor, time has stopped for and around him: if he lives there (*pointing to Frida*) with her, eight hundred years ago . . . I repeat: the giddiness of the jump will be such, that finding himself suddenly among us . . . (*The doctor shakes his head in dissent*). You don't think so?

DOCTOR. No, because life, my dear baron, can take up its rhythms. This—our life—will at once become real also to him; and will pull him up directly, wresting from him suddenly the illusion, and showing him that the eight hundred years, as you say, are only twenty! It will be like one of those tricks, such as the leap into space, for instance, of the Masonic rite, which appears to be heaven knows how far, and is only a step down the stairs.

BELCREDI. Ah! An idea! Yes! Look at Frida and the Marchioness, doctor! Which is more advanced in time? We old people, doctor! The young ones think they are more ahead; but it isn't true: we are more ahead, because time belongs to us more than to them.

DOCTOR. If the past didn't alienate us . . .

BELCREDI. It doesn't matter at all! How does it alienate us? They (*pointing to Frida and Di Nolli*) have still to do what we have accomplished, doctor: to grow old, doing the same foolish things, more or less, as we did . . . This is the illusion: that one comes forward through a door to life. It isn't so! As soon as one is born, one starts dying; therefore, he who started first is the most advanced of all. The youngest of us is father Adam! Look there: (*pointing to Frida*) eight hundred years younger than all of us—the Countess Matilda of Tuscany. (*He makes her a deep bow*).

DI NOLLI. I say, Tito, don't start joking.

BELCREDI. Oh, you think I am joking? . . .

DI NOLLI. Of course, of course . . . all the time.

BELCREDI. Impossible! I've even dressed up as a Benedictine . . .

DI NOLLI. Yes, but for a serious purpose.

BELCREDI. Well, exactly. If it has been serious for the

[Act II]   *"HENRY IV."*   119

others . . . for Frida, now, for instance. (*Then turning to the doctor*): I swear, doctor, I don't yet understand what you want to do.

DOCTOR (*annoyed*). You'll see! Let me do as I wish . . . At present you see the Marchioness still dressed as . . .

BELCREDI. Oh, she also . . . has to masquerade?

DOCTOR. Of course! of course! In another dress that's in there ready to be used when it comes into his head he sees the Countess Matilda of Canossa before him.

FRIDA (*while talking quietly to Di Nolli notices the doctor's mistake*). Of Tuscany, of Tuscany!

DOCTOR. It's all the same!

BELCREDI. Oh, I see! He'll be faced by two of them . . .

DOCTOR. Two, precisely! And then . . .

FRIDA (*calling him aside*). Come here, doctor! Listen!

DOCTOR. Here I am! (*Goes near the two young people and pretends to give some explanations to them*).

BELCREDI (*softly to Donna Matilda*). I say, this is getting rather strong, you know!

DONNA MATILDA (*looking him firmly in the face*). What?

BELCREDI. Does it really interest you as much as all that—to make you willing to take part in . . . ? For a woman, this is simply enormous! . . .

DONNA MATILDA. Yes, for an ordinary woman.

BELCREDI. Oh, no, my dear, for all women,—in a question like this! It's an abnegation.

DONNA MATILDA. I owe it to him.

BELCREDI. Don't lie! You know well enough it's not hurting you!

DONNA MATILDA. Well then, where does the abnegation come in?

BELCREDI. Just enough to prevent you losing caste in other people's eyes—and just enough to offend me! . . .

DONNA MATILDA. But who is worrying about you now?

DI NOLLI (*coming forward*). It's all right. It's all right. That's what we'll do! (*Turning towards Berthold*): Here you, go and call one of those fellows!

BERTHOLD. At once! (*Exit*).

DONNA MATILDA. But first of all we've got to pretend that we are going away.

DI NOLLI. Exactly! I'll see to that . . . (*to Belcredi*) you don't mind staying here?

BELCREDI (*ironically*). Oh, no, I don't mind, I don't mind! . . .

DI NOLLI. We must look out not to make him suspicious again, you know.

BELCREDI. Oh, Lord! *He* doesn't amount to anything!

DOCTOR. He must believe absolutely that we've gone away. (*Landolph followed by Berthold enters from the right*).

LANDOLPH. May I come in?

DI NOLLI. Come in! Come in! I say—your name's Lolo, isn't it?

LANDOLPH. Lolo, or Landolph, just as you like!

DI NOLLI. Well, look here: the doctor and the Marchioness are leaving, at once.

LANDOLPH. Very well. All we've got to say is that they have been able to obtain the permission for the reception from His Holiness. He's in there in his own apartments repenting of all he said—and in an awful state to have the pardon! Would you mind coming a minute? . . . If you would, just for a minute . . . put on the dress again . . .

DOCTOR. Why, of course, with pleasure . . .

LANDOLPH. Might I be allowed to make a suggestion? Why not add that the Marchioness of Tuscany has interceded with the Pope that he should be received?

DONNA MATILDA. You see, he has recognized me!

LANDOLPH. Forgive me ... I don't know my history very well. I am sure you gentlemen know it much better! But I thought it was believed that Henry IV. had a secret passion for the Marchioness of Tuscany.

DONNA MATILDA (*at once*). Nothing of the kind! Nothing of the kind!

LANDOLPH. That's what I thought! But he says he's loved her ... he's always saying it ... And now he fears that her indignation for this secret love of his will work him harm with the Pope.

BELCREDI. We must let him understand that this aversion no longer exists.

LANDOLPH. Exactly! Of course!

DONNA MATILDA (*to Belcredi*). History says—I don't know whether you know it or not—that the Pope gave way to the supplications of the Marchioness Matilda and the Abbot of Cluny. And I may say, my dear Belcredi, that I intended to take advantage of this fact—at the time of the pageant—to show him my feelings were not so hostile to him as he supposed.

BELCREDI. You are most faithful to history, Marchioness ...

LANDOLPH. Well then, the Marchioness could spare herself a double disguise and present herself with Monsignor (*indicating the doctor*) as the Marchioness of Tuscany.

DOCTOR (*quickly, energetically*). No, no! That won't do at all. It would ruin everything. The impression from the confrontation must be a sudden one, give a shock! No, no, Marchioness, you will appear again as the Duchess Adelaide, the mother of the Empress. And then we'll go away. This is most necessary: that he should know we've gone away. Come on! Don't let's waste any more time! There's a lot to prepare.

(*Exeunt the doctor, Donna Matilda, and Landolph, right*).

FRIDA. I am beginning to feel afraid again.

DI NOLLI. Again, Frida?

FRIDA. It would have been better if I had seen him before.

DI NOLLI. There's nothing to be frightened of, really.

FRIDA. He isn't furious, is he?

DI NOLLI. Of course not! he's quite calm.

BELCREDI (*with ironic sentimental affectation*). Melancholy! Didn't you hear that he loves you?

FRIDA. Thanks! That's just why I am afraid.

BELCREDI. He won't do you any harm.

DI NOLLI. It'll only last a minute . . .

FRIDA. Yes, but there in the dark with him . . .

DI NOLLI. Only for a moment; and I will be near you, and all the others behind the door ready to run in. As soon as you see your mother, your part will be finished . . .

BELCREDI. I'm afraid of a different thing: that we're wasting our time . . .

DI NOLLI. Don't begin again! The remedy seems a sound one to me.

FRIDA. I think so too! I feel it! I'm all trembling!

BELCREDI. But, mad people, my dear friends—though they don't know it, alas—have this felicity which we don't take into account . . .

DI NOLLI (*interrupting, annoyed*). What felicity? Nonsense!

BELCREDI (*forcefully*). They don't reason!

DI NOLLI. What's reasoning got to do with it, anyway?

BELCREDI. Don't you call it reasoning that he will have to do—according to us—when he sees her (*indicates Frida*) and her mother? We've reasoned it all out, surely!

DI NOLLI. Nothing of the kind: no reasoning at all!

We put before him a double image of his own fantasy, or fiction, as the doctor says.

BELCREDI (*suddenly*). I say, I've never understood why they take degrees in medicine.

DI NOLLI (*amazed*). Who?

BELCREDI. The alienists!

DI NOLLI. What ought they to take degrees in, then?

FRIDA. If they are alienists, in what else should they take degrees?

BELCREDI. In law, of course! All a matter of talk! The more they talk, the more highly they are considered. "Analogous elasticity," "the sensation of distance in time!" And the first thing they tell you is that they don't work miracles— when a miracle's just what is wanted! But they know that the more they say they are not miracle-workers, the more folk believe in their seriousness!

BERTHOLD (*who has been looking through the keyhole of the door on right*). There they are! There they are! They're coming in here.

DI NOLLI. Are they?

BERTHOLD. He wants to come with them . . . Yes! . . . He's coming too!

DI NOLLI. Let's get away, then! Let's get away, at once! (*To Berthold*): You stop here!

BERTHOLD. Must I?

(*Without answering him, Di Nolli, Frida, and Belcredi go out by the main exit, leaving Berthold surprised. The door on the right opens, and Landolph enters first, bowing. Then Donna Matilda comes in, with mantle and ducal crown as in the first act; also the doctor as the abbot of Cluny. Henry IV. is among them in royal dress. Ordulph and Harold enter last of all*).

HENRY IV. (*following up what he has been saying in the*

other room). And now I will ask you a question: how can I be astute, if you think me obstinate?

DOCTOR. No, no, not obstinate!

HENRY IV. (*smiling, pleased*). Then you think me really astute?

DOCTOR. No, no, neither obstinate, nor astute.

HENRY IV. (*with benevolent irony*). Monsignor, if obstinacy is not a vice which can go with astuteness, I hoped that in denying me the former, you would at least allow me a little of the latter. I can assure you I have great need of it. But if you want to keep it all for yourself . . .

DOCTOR. I? I? Do I seem astute to you?

HENRY IV. No. Monsignor! What do you say? Not in the least! Perhaps in this case, I may seem a little obstinate to you (*cutting short to speak to Donna Matilda*). With your permission: a word in confidence to the Duchess. (*Leads her aside and asks her very earnestly*): Is your daughter really dear to you?

DONNA MATILDA (*dismayed*). Why, yes, certainly . . .

HENRY IV. Do you wish me to compensate her with all my love, with all my devotion, for the grave wrongs I have done her—though you must not believe all the stories my enemies tell about my dissoluteness!

DONNA MATILDA. No, no, I don't believe them. I never have believed such stories.

HENRY IV. Well, then are you willing?

DONNA MATILDA (*confused*). What?

HENRY IV. That I return to love your daughter again? (*Looks at her and adds, in a mysterious tone of warning*). You mustn't be a friend of the Marchioness of Tuscany!

DONNA MATILDA. I tell you again that she has begged and tried not less than ourselves to obtain your pardon . . .

HENRY IV. (*softly, but excitedly*). Don't tell me that!

[Act II] "HENRY IV." 125

Don't say that to me! Don't you see the effect it has on me, my Lady?

DONNA MATILDA (*looks at him; then very softly as if in confidence*). You love her still?

HENRY IV. (*puzzled*). Still? Still, you say? You know, then? But nobody knows! Nobody must know!

DONNA MATILDA. But perhaps she knows, if she has begged so hard for you!

HENRY IV. (*looks at her and says*): And you love your daughter? (*Brief pause. He turns to the doctor with laughing accents*). Ah, Monsignor, it's strange how little I think of my wife! It may be a sin, but I swear to you that I hardly feel her at all in my heart. What is stranger is that her own mother scarcely feels her in her heart. Confess, my Lady, that she amounts to very little for you. (*Turning to Doctor*): She talks to me of that other woman, insistently, insistently, I don't know why! . . .

LANDOLPH (*humbly*). Maybe, Majesty, it is to disabuse you of some ideas you have had about the Marchioness of Tuscany. (*Then, dismayed at having allowed himself this observation, adds*): I mean just now, of course . . .

HENRY IV. You too maintain that she has been friendly to me?

LANDOLPH. Yes, at the moment, Majesty.

DONNA MATILDA. Exactly! Exactly! . . .

HENRY IV. I understand. That is to say, you don't believe I love her. I see! I see! Nobody's ever believed it, nobody's ever thought it. Better so, then! But enough, enough! (*Turns to the doctor with changed expression*): Monsignor, you see? The reasons the Pope has had for revoking the excommunication have got nothing at all to do with the reasons for which he excommunicated me originally. Tell Pope Gregory we shall meet again at Brixen. And you, Madame, should you chance to meet your daughter in the courtyard of the castle of your friend the Marchioness, ask her to visit me. We shall see if I succeed in keeping her close beside me as wife and Empress. Many women have presented themselves here already assuring me that they were she. But they all, even while they told me they came from Susa—I don't know why—began to laugh! And then in the bedroom . . . Well a man is a man, and a woman is a woman. Undressed, we don't bother much about who we are. And one's dress is like a phantom that hovers always near one. Oh, Monsignor, phantoms in general are nothing more than trifling disorders of the spirit: images we cannot contain within the bounds of sleep. They reveal themselves even when we are awake, and they frighten us. I . . . ah . . . I am always afraid when, at night time, I see disordered images before me. Sometimes I am even afraid of my own blood pulsing loudly in my arteries in the silence of night, like the sound of a distant step in a lonely corridor! . . . But, forgive me! I have kept you standing too long already. I thank you, my Lady, I thank you, Monsignor. (*Donna Matilda and the Doctor go off bowing. As soon as they have gone, Henry IV. suddenly changes his tone*). Buffoons, buffoons! One can play any tune on them! And that other fellow . . . Pietro Damiani! . . . Caught him out perfectly! He's afraid to appear before me again. (*Moves up and down excitedly while saying this; then sees Berthold, and points him out to the other three valets*). Oh, look at this imbecile watching me with his mouth wide open! (*Shakes him*). Don't you understand? Don't you see, idiot, how I treat them, how I play the fool with them, make them appear before me just as I wish? Miserable, frightened clowns that they are! And you (*addressing the valets*) are amazed that I tear off their ridiculous masks now, just as if it wasn't I who had made them mask themselves to satisfy this taste of mine for playing the madman!

LANDOLPH—HAROLD—ORDULPH (*bewildered, looking at one another*). What? What does he say? What?

HENRY IV. (*answers them imperiously*). Enough! enough! Let's stop it. I'm tired of it. (*Then as if the thought left him no peace*): By God! The impudence! To come here along with her lover! . . . And pretending to do it out of pity! So as not to infuriate a poor devil already out of the world, out of time, out of life! If it hadn't been supposed to be done out of pity, one can well imagine that fellow wouldn't have allowed it. Those people expect others to behave as they wish all the time. And, of course, there's nothing arrogant in that! Oh, no! Oh, no! It's merely their way of thinking, of feeling, of seeing. Everybody has his own way of thinking; you fellows, too. Yours is that of a flock of sheep—miserable, feeble, uncertain . . . But those others take advantage of this and make you accept their way of thinking; or, at least, they suppose they do; Because, after all, what do they succeed in imposing on you? Words, words which anyone can interpret in his own manner! That's the way public opinion is formed! And it's a bad look out for a man who finds himself labelled one day with one of these words which everyone repeats; for example "madman," or "imbecile." Don't you think is rather hard for a man to keep quiet, when he knows that there is a fellow going about trying to persuade everybody that he is as he sees him, trying to fix him in other people's opinion as a "madman"—according to him? Now I am talking seriously! Before I hurt my head, falling from my horse . . . (*stops suddenly, noticing the dismay of the four young men*). What's the matter with you? (*Imitates their amazed looks*). What? Am I, or am I not, mad? Oh, yes! I'm mad all right! (*He becomes terrible*). Well, then, by God, down on your knees, down on your knees! (*Makes them go down on their knees one by one*). I order you to go down on your knees before me! And touch the ground three times with your foreheads! Down, down! That's the way you've got to be before madmen! (*Then annoyed with their facile humiliation*): Get up, sheep! You obeyed me, didn't you? You might have put the straight jacket on me! . . . Crush a man with the weight of a word—it's nothing —a fly! all our life is crushed by the weight of words: the weight of the dead. Look at me here: can you really suppose that Henry IV. is still alive? All the same, I speak, and order you live men about! Do you think it's a joke that the dead continue to live?—Yes, *here* it's a joke! But get out into the live world!—Ah, you say: what a beautiful sunrise—for us! All time is before us!—Dawn! We will do what we like with this day—. Ah, yes! To Hell with tradition, the old conventions! Well, go on! You will do nothing but repeat the old, old words, while you imagine you are living! (*Goes up to Berthold who has now become quite stupid*). You don't understand a word of this, do you? What's your name?

BERTHOLD. I? . . . What? . . . Berthold . . .

HENRY IV. Poor Berthold! What's your name here?

BERTHOLD. I . . . I . . . my name in Fino.

HENRY IV. (*feeling the warning and critical glances of the others, turns to them to reduce them to silence*). Fino?

BERTHOLD. Fino Pagliuca, sire.

HENRY IV. (*turning to Landolph*). I've heard you call each other by your nick-names often enough! Your name is Lolo, isn't it?

LANDOLPH. Yes, sire . . . (*then with a sense of immense joy*). Oh, Lord! Oh Lord! Then he is not mad . . . .

HENRY IV. (*brusquely*). What?

LANDOLPH (*hesitating*). No . . . I said . . .

HENRY IV. Not mad, eh? We're having a joke on those

that think I am mad! (*To Harold*)—I say, boy, your name's Franco . . . (*to Ordulph*) And yours . . .

ORDULPH. Momo.

HENRY IV. Momo, Momo . . . A nice name that!

LANDOLPH. So he isn't . . .

HENRY IV. What are you talking about? Of course not! Let's have a jolly, good laugh! . . . (*Laughs*): Ah! . . . Ah! . . . Ah! . . .

LANDOLPH—HAROLD—ORDULPH (*looking at each other half happy and half dismayed*). Then he's cured! . . . he's all right! . . .

HENRY IV. Silence! Silence! . . . (*To Berthold*): Why don't you laugh? Are you offended? I didn't mean it especially for you. It's convenient for everybody to insist that certain people are mad, so they can be shut up. Do you know why? Because it's impossible to hear them speak! What shall I say of these people who've just gone away? That one is a whore, another a libertine, another a swindler . . . don't you think so? You can't believe a word he says . . . don't you think so?—By the way, they all listen to me terrified. And why are they terrified, if what I say isn't true? Of course, you can't believe what madmen say—yet, at the same time, they stand there with their eyes wide open with terror!—Why? Tell me, tell me, why?—You see I'm quite calm now!

BERTHOLD. But, perhaps, they think that . . .

HENRY IV. No, no, my dear fellow! Look me well in the eyes! . . . I don't say that it's true—nothing is true, Berthold! But . . . look me in the eyes!

BERTHOLD. Well . . .

HENRY IV. You see? You see? . . . You have terror in your own eyes now because I seem mad to you! There's the proof of it (*laughs*)!

LANDOLPH (*coming forward in the name of the others, exasperated*). What proof?

HENRY IV. Your being so dismayed because now I seem again mad to you. You have thought me mad up to now, haven't you? You feel that this dismay of yours can become terror too—something to dash away the ground from under your feet and deprive you of the air you breathe! Do you know what it means to find yourselves face to face with a madman—with one who shakes the foundations of all you have built up in yourselves, your logic, the logic of all your constructions? Madmen, lucky folk! construct without logic, or rather with a logic that flies like a feather. Voluble! Voluble! Today like this and tomorrow — who knows? You say: "This cannot be"; but for them everything can be. You say: "This isn't true!" And why? Because it doesn't seem true to you, or you, or you . . . (*indicates the three of them in succession*) . . . and to a hundred thousand others! One must see what seems true to these hundred thousand others who are not supposed to be mad! What a magnificent spectacle they afford, when they reason! What flowers of logic they scatter! I know that when I was a child, I thought the moon in the pond was real. How many things I thought real! I believed everything I was told—and I was happy! Because it's a terrible thing if you don't hold on to that which seems true to you today—to that which will seem true to you tomorrow, even if it is the opposite of that which seemed true to you yesterday. I would never wish you to think, as I have done, on this horrible thing which really drives one mad: that if you were beside another and looking into his eyes—as I one day looked into somebody's eyes—you might as well be a beggar before a door never to be opened to you; for he who does enter there will never be you, but someone unknown to you with his own different and impenetrable world . . . (*Long pause. Dark-*

ness gathers in the room, increasing the sense of strangeness and consternation in which the four young men are involved. Henry IV remains aloof, pondering on the misery which is not only his, but everybody's. Then he pulls himself up, and says in an ordinary tone): It's getting dark here . . .

ORDULPH. Shall I go for a lamp?

HENRY IV. (*Ironically*). The lamp, yes the lamp! . . . Do you suppose I don't know that as soon as I turn my back with my oil lamp to go to bed, you turn on the electric light for yourselves, here, and even there, in the throne room? I pretend not to see it!

ORDULPH. Well, then, shall I turn it on now?

HENRY IV. No, it would blind me! I want my lamp!

ORDULPH. It's ready here behind the door. (*Goes to the main exit, opens the door, goes out for a moment, and returns with an ancient lamp which is held by a ring at the top*).

HENRY IV. Ah, a little light! Sit there around the table, no, not like that; in an elegant, easy, manner! . . . (*To Harold*): Yes, you, like that (*poses him*)! (*Then to Berthold*): You, so! . . . and I, here (*sits opposite them*)! We could do with a little decorative moonlight. It's very useful for us, the moonlight. I feel a real necessity for it, and pass a lot of time looking up at the moon from my window. Who would think, to look at her that she knows that eight hundred years have passed, and that I, seated at the window, cannot really be Henry IV gazing at the moon like any poor devil? But, look, look! See what a magnificent night scene we have here: the emperor surrounded by his faithful counsellors! . . . How do you like it?

LANDOLPH (*softly to Harold, so as not to break the enchantment*). And to think it wasn't true! . . .

HENRY IV. True? What wasn't true?

LANDOLPH (*timidly as if to excuse himself*). No . . . I mean . . . I was saying this morning to him (*indicates Berthold*)—he has just entered on service here—I was saying: what a pity that dressed like this and with so many beautiful costumes in the wardrobe . . . and with a room like that (*indicates the throne room*) . . .

HENRY IV. Well? what's the pity?

LANDOLPH. Well . . . that we didn't know . . .

HENRY IV. That it was all done in jest, this comedy?

LANDOLPH. Because we thought that . . .

HAROLD (*coming to his assistance*). Yes . . . that it was done seriously!

HENRY IV. What do you say? Doesn't it seem serious to you?

LANDOLPH. But if you say that . . .

HENRY IV. I say that—you are fools! You ought to have known how to create a fantasy for yourselves, not to act it for me, or anyone coming to see me; but naturally, simply, day by day, before nobody, feeling yourselves alive in the history of the eleventh century, here at the court of your emperor, Henry IV! You Ordulph (*taking him by the arm*), alive in the castle of Goslar, waking up in the morning, getting out of bed, and entering straightway into the dream, clothing yourself in the dream that would be no more a dream, because you would have lived it, felt it all alive in you. You would have drunk it in with the air you breathed; yet knowing all the time that it was a dream, so you could better enjoy the privilege afforded you of having to do nothing else but live this dream, this far off and yet actual dream! And to think that at a distance of eight centuries from this remote age of ours, so coloured and so sepulchral, the men of the twentieth century are torturing themselves in ceaseless anxiety to know how their fates and fortunes will work out! Whereas you are already in history with me . . .

LANDOLPH. Yes, yes, very good!

HENRY IV. . . . Everything determined, everything settled!

ORDULPH. Yes, yes!

HENRY IV. And sad as is my lot, hideous as some of the events are, bitter the struggles and troublous the time—still all history! All history that cannot change, understand? All fixed for ever! And you could have admired at your ease how every effect followed obediently its cause with perfect logic, how every event took place precisely and coherently in each minute particular! The pleasure, the pleasure of history, in fact, which is so great, was yours.

LANDOLPH. Beautiful, beautiful!

HENRY IV. Beautiful, but it's finished! Now that you know, I could not do it any more! (*Takes his lamp to go to bed*). Neither could you, if up to now you haven't understood the reason of it! I am sick of it now. (*Almost to himself with violent contained rage*): By God, I'll make her sorry she came here! Dressed herself up as a mother-in-law for me . . . ! And he as an abbot . . . ! And they bring a doctor with them to study me . . . ! Who knows if they don't hope to cure me? . . . Clowns . . . ! I'd like to smack one of them at least in the face: yes, that one—a famous swordsman, they say! . . . He'll kill me . . . Well, we'll see, we'll see! . . . (*A knock at the door*). Who is it?

THE VOICE OF JOHN. Deo Gratias!

HAROLD (*very pleased at the chance for another joke*). Oh, it's John, it's old John, who comes every night to play the monk.

ORDULPH (*rubbing his hands*). Yes, yes! Let's make him do it!

HENRY IV. (*at once, severely*). Fool, why? Just to play a joke on a poor old man who does it for love of me?

LANDOLPH (*to Ordulph*). It has to be as if it were true.

HENRY IV. Exactly, as if true! Because, only so, truth is not a jest (*opens the door and admits John dressed as a humble friar with a roll of parchment under his arm*). Come in, come in, father! (*Then assuming a tone of tragic gravity and deep resentment*): All the documents of my life and reign favorable to me were destroyed deliberately by my enemies. One only has escaped destruction, this, my life, written by a humble monk who is devoted to me. And you would laugh at him! (*Turns affectionately to John, and invites him to sit down at the table*). Sit down, father, sit down! Have the lamp near you (*puts the lamp near him*)! Write! Write!

JOHN (*opens the parchment and prepares to write from dictation*). I am ready, your Majesty!

HENRY IV. (*dictating*). "The decree of peace proclaimed at Mayence helped the poor and humble, while it damaged the weak and the powerful (*curtain begins to fall*): It brought wealth to the former, hunger and misery to the latter . . ."

Curtain.

ACT III

The throne room so dark that the wall at the bottom is hardly seen. The canvasses of the two portraits have been taken away; and, within their frames, Frida, dressed as the "Marchioness of Tuscany" and Charles Di Nolli, as "Henry IV.," have taken the exact positions of the portraits.

For a moment, after the raising of curtain, the stage is empty. Then the door on the left opens; and Henry IV., holding the lamp by the ring on top of it, enters. He looks back to speak to the four young men who, with John, are presumedly in the adjoining hall, as at the end of the second act.

HENRY IV. No: stay where you are, stay where you are. I shall manage all right by myself. Good night! (*Closes the door and walks, very sad and tired, across the hall towards the second door on the right, which leads into his apartments*).

FRIDA (*as soon as she sees that he has just passed the throne, whispers from the niche like one who is on the point of fainting away with fright*). Henry . . .

HENRY IV. (*stopping at the voice, as if someone had stabbed him traitorously in the back, turns a terror-stricken face towards the wall at the bottom of the room; raising an arm instinctively, as if to defend himself and ward off a blow*). Who is calling me? (*It is not a question, but an exclamation vibrating with terror, which does not expect a reply from the darkness and the terrible silence of the hall, which suddenly fills him with the suspicion that he is really mad*).

FRIDA (*at his shudder of terror, is herself not less*

frightened at the part she is playing, and repeats a little more loudly). Henry! . . . (*But, although she wishes to act the part as they have given it to her, she stretches her head a little out of the frame towards the other frame*).

HENRY IV. (*Gives a dreadful cry; lets the lamp fall from his hands to cover his head with his arms, and makes a movement as if to run away*).

FRIDA (*jumping from the frame on to the stand and shouting like a mad woman*). Henry! . . . Henry! . . . I'm afraid! . . . I'm terrified! . . .

(*And while Di Nolli jumps in turn on to the stand and thence to the floor and runs to Frida who, on the verge of fainting, continues to cry out, the Doctor, Donna Matilda, also dressed as "Matilda of Tuscany," Tito Belcredi, Landolph, Berthold and John enter the hall from the doors on the right and on the left. One of them turns on the light: a strange light coming from lamps hidden in the ceiling so that only the upper part of the stage is well lighted. The others without taking notice of Henry IV, who looks on astonished by the unexpected inrush, after the moment of terror which still causes him to tremble, run anxiously to support and comfort the still shaking Frida, who is moaning in the arms of her fiancé. All are speaking at the same time.*)

DI NOLLI. No, no, Frida . . . Here I am . . . I am beside you!

DOCTOR (*coming with the others*). Enough! Enough! There's nothing more to be done! . . .

DONNA MATILDA. He is cured, Frida. Look! He is cured! Don't you see?

DI NOLLI (*astonished*). Cured?

BELCREDI. It was only for fun! Be calm!

FRIDA. No! I am afraid! I am afraid!

DONNA MATILDA. Afraid of what? Look at him! He was never mad at all! . . .

DI NOLLI. That isn't true! What are you saying? Cured?

DOCTOR. It appears so. I should say so . . .

BELCREDI. Yes, yes! They have told us so (*pointing to the four young men*).

DONNA MATILDA. Yes, for a long time! He has confided in them, told them the truth!

DI NOLLI (*now more indignant than astonished*). But what does it mean? If, up to a short time ago . . . ?

BELCREDI. Hum! He was acting, to take you in and also us, who in good faith . . .

DI NOLLI. Is it possible? To deceive his sister, also, right up to the time of her death?

HENRY IV. (*Remains apart, peering at one and now at the other under the accusation and the mockery of what all believe to be a cruel joke of his, which is now revealed. He has shown by the flashing of his eyes that he is meditating a revenge, which his violent contempt prevents him from defining clearly, as yet. Stung to the quick and with a clear idea of accepting the fiction they have insidiously worked up as true, he bursts forth at this point*): Go on, I say! Go on!

DI NOLLI (*astonished at the cry*). Go on! What do you mean?

HENRY IV. It isn't *your* sister only that is dead!

DI NOLLI. My sister? Yours, I say, whom you compelled up to the last moment, to present herself here as your mother Agnes!

HENRY IV. And was she not *your* mother?

DI NOLLI. My mother? Certainly my mother!

HENRY IV. But your mother is dead for me, *old and far away*! You have just got down now from there (*pointing to the frame from which he jumped down*). And how do you know whether I have not wept her long in secret, dressed even as I am?

Donna Matilda (*dismayed, looking at the others*). What does he say? (*Much impressed, observing him*). Quietly! quietly, for Heaven's sake!

Henry IV. What do I say? I ask all of you if Agnes was not the mother of Henry IV? (*Turns to Frida as if she were really the Marchioness of Tuscany*): You, Marchioness, it seems to me, ought to know.

Frida (*still frightened, draws closer to Di Nolli*). No, no, I don't know. Not I!

Doctor. It's the madness returning. . . . Quiet now, everybody!

Belcredi (*indignant*). Madness indeed, doctor! He's acting again! . . .

Henry IV. (*suddenly*). I? You have emptied those two frames over there, and he stands before my eyes as Henry IV. . . .

Belcredi. We've had enough of this joke now.

Henry IV. Who said joke?

Doctor (*loudly to Belcredi*). Don't excite him, for the love of God!

Belcredi (*without lending an ear to him, but speaking louder*). But they have said so (*pointing again to the four young men*), they, they!

Henry IV. (*turning round and looking at them*). You? Did you say it was all a joke?

Landolph (*timid and embarrassed*). No . . . really we said that you were cured.

Belcredi. Look here! Enough of this! (*To Donna Matilda*): Doesn't it seem to you that the sight of him (*pointing to Di Nolli*), Marchioness and that of your daughter dressed so, is becoming an intolerable puerility?

Donna Matilda. Oh, be quiet! What does the dress matter, if he is cured?

Henry IV. Cured, yes! I am cured! (*To Belcredi*) ah,

but not to let it end this way all at once, as you suppose! (*Attacks him*). Do you know that for twenty years nobody has ever dared to appear before me here like you and that gentleman (*pointing to the doctor*)?

BELCREDI. Of course I know it. As a matter of fact, I too appeared before you this morning dressed . . .

HENRY IV. As a monk, yes!

BELCREDI. And you took me for Peter Damiani! And I didn't even laugh, believing, in fact, that . . .

HENRY IV. That I was mad! Does it make you laugh seeing her like that, now that I am cured? And yet you might have remembered that in my eyes her appearance now . . . (*interrupts himself with a gesture of contempt*) Ah! (*Suddenly turns to the doctor*): You are a doctor, aren't you?

DOCTOR. Yes.

HENRY IV. And you also took part in dressing her up as the Marchioness of Tuscany? To prepare a counter-joke for me here, eh?

DONNA MATILDA (*impetuously*). No, no! What do you say? It was done for you! I did it for your sake.

DOCTOR (*quickly*). To attempt, to try, not knowing . . .

HENRY IV. (*cutting him short*). I understand. I say counter-joke, in his case (*indicates Belcredi*), because he believes that I have been carrying on a jest . . .

BELCREDI. But excuse me, what do you mean? You say yourself you are cured.

HENRY IV. Let me speak! (*To the doctor*): Do you know, doctor, that for a moment you ran the risk of making me mad again? By God, to make the portraits speak; to make them jump alive out of their frames . . .

DOCTOR. But you saw that all of us ran in at once, as soon as they told us . . .

HENRY IV. Certainly! (*Contemplates Frida and Di*

Nolli, and then looks at the Marchioness, and finally at his own costume). The combination is very beautiful . . . Two couples . . . Very good, very good, doctor! For a madman, not bad! . . . (*With a slight wave of his hand to Belcredi*): It seems to him now to be a carnival out of season, eh? (*Turns to look at him*). We'll get rid now of this masquerade costume of mine, so that I may come away with you. What do you say?

BELCREDI. With me? With us?

HENRY IV. Where shall we go? To the Club? In dress coats and with white ties? Or shall both of us go to the Marchioness' house?

BELCREDI. Wherever you like! Do you want to remain here still, to continue—alone—what was nothing but the unfortunate joke of a day of carnival? It is really incredible, incredible how you have been able to do all this, freed from the disaster that befell you!

HENRY IV. Yes, you see how it was! The fact is that falling from my horse and striking my head as I did, I was really mad for I know not how long . . .

DOCTOR. Ah! Did it last long?

HENRY IV. (*very quickly to the doctor*). Yes, doctor, a long time! I think it must have been about twelve years. (*Then suddenly turning to speak to Belcredi*): Thus I saw nothing, my dear fellow, of all that, after that day of carnival, happened for you but not for me: how things changed, how my friends deceived me, how my place was taken by another, and all the rest of it! And suppose my place had been taken in the heart of the woman I loved? . . . And how should I know who was dead or who had disappeared? . . . All this, you know, wasn't exactly a jest for me, as it seems to you . . .

BELCREDI. No, no! I don't mean that if you please. I mean after . . .

HENRY IV. Ah, yes? After? One day (*stops and addresses the doctor*)—A most interesting case, doctor! Study me well! Study me carefully (*trembles while speaking*)! All by itself, who knows how, one day the trouble here (*touches his forehead*) mended. Little by little, I open my eyes, and at first I don't know whether I am asleep or awake. Then I know I am awake. I touch this thing and that; I see clearly again . . . Ah!—then, as *he* says (*alludes to Belcredi*) away, away with this masquerade, this incubus! Let's open the windows, breathe life once again! Away! Away! Let's run out! (*Suddenly pulling himself up*). But where? And to do what? To show myself to all, secretly, as Henry IV., not like this, but arm in arm with you, among my dear friends?

BELCREDI. What are you saying?

DONNA MATILDA. Who could think it? It's not to be imagined. It was an accident.

HENRY IV. They all said I was mad before. (*To Belcredi*): And you know it! You were more ferocious than any one against those who tried to defend me.

BELCREDI. Oh, that was only a joke!

HENRY IV. Look at my hair! (*Shows him the hair on the nape of his neck*).

BELCREDI. But mine is grey too!

HENRY IV. Yes, with this difference: that mine went grey here, as Henry IV., do you understand? And I never knew it! I perceived it all of a sudden, one day, when I opened my eyes; and I was terrified because I understood at once that not only had my hair gone grey, but that I was all grey, inside; that everything had fallen to pieces, that everything was finished; and I was going to arrive, hungry as a wolf, at a banquet which had already been cleared away . . .

BELCREDI. Yes, but, what about the others? . . .

HENRY IV. (*quickly*). Ah, yes, I know! They couldn't

wait until I was cured, not even those, who, behind my back, pricked my saddled horse till it bled. . . .

DI NOLLI (*agitated*). What, what?

HENRY IV. Yes, treacherously, to make it rear and cause me to fall.

DONNA MATILDA (*quickly, in horror*). This is the first time I knew that.

HENRY IV. That was also a joke, probably!

DONNA MATILDA. But who did it? Who was behind us, then?

HENRY IV. It doesn't matter who it was. All those that went on feasting and were ready to leave me their scrapings, Marchioness, of miserable pity, or some dirty remnant of remorse in the filthy plate! Thanks! (*Turning quickly to the doctor*): Now doctor, the case must be absolutely new in the history of madness; I preferred to remain mad—since I found everything ready and at my disposal for this new exquisite fantasy. I would live it—this madness of mine—with the most lucid consciousness; and thus revenge myself on the brutality of a stone which had dinted my head. The solitude—this solitude—squalid and empty as it appeared to me when I opened my eyes again—I determined to deck it out with all the colours and splendors of that far off day of carnival, when you (*looks at Donna Matilda and points Frida out to her*) when you, Marchioness, triumphed. So I would oblige all those who were around me to follow, by God, at my orders that famous pageant which had been— for you and not for me—the jest of a day. I would make it become—for ever—no more a joke but a reality, the reality of a real madness: here, all in masquerade, with throne room, and these my four secret counsellors: secret and, of course, traitors. (*He turns quickly towards them*). I should like to know what you have gained by revealing the fact that I was cured! If I am cured, there's no longer any need of you, and you will be discharged! To give anyone one's confidence . . . that is really the act of a madman. But now I accuse you in my turn (*turning to the others*)! Do you know? They thought (*alludes to the valets*) they could make fun of me too with you (*bursts out laughing. The others laugh, but shamefacedly, except Donna Matilda*).

BELCREDI (*to Di Nolli*). Well, imagine that .'. . That's not bad . . .

DI NOLLI (*to the four young men*). You?

HENRY IV. We must pardon them. This dress (*plucking his dress*) which is for me the evident, involuntary caricature of that other continuous, everlasting masquerade, of which we are the involuntary puppets (*indicates Belcredi*), when, without knowing it, we mask ourselves with that which we appear to be . . . ah, that dress of theirs, this masquerade of theirs, of course, we must forgive it them, since they do not yet see it is identical with themselves . . . (*Turning again to Belcredi*): You know, it is quite easy to get accustomed to it. One walks about as a tragic character, just as if it were nothing . . . (*Imitates the tragic manner*) in a room like this . . . Look here, doctor! I remember a priest, certainly Irish, a nice-looking priest, who was sleeping in the sun one November day, with his arm on the corner of the bench of a public garden. He was lost in the golden delight of the mild sunny air which must have seemed for him almost summery. One may be sure that in that moment he did not know any more that he was a priest, or even where he was. He was dreaming . . . A little boy passed with a flower in his hand. He touched the priest with it here on the neck. I saw him open his laughing eyes, while all his mouth smiled with the beauty of his dream. He was forgetful of everything . . . But all at once, he pulled himself together, and stretched out his priest's cassock; and there came back to his eyes the same seriousness which you have seen in mine; because the Irish priests defend the seriousness of their Catholic faith with the same zeal with which I defend the secret rights of hereditary monarchy! I am cured, gentlemen: because I can act the mad man to perfection, here; and I do it very quietly, I'm only sorry for you that have to live your madness so agitatedly, without knowing it or seeing it.

BELCREDI. It comes to this, then, that it is we who are mad. That's what it is!

HENRY IV. (*containing his irritation*). But if you weren't mad, both you and she (*indicating the Marchioness*) would you have come here to see me?

BELCREDI. To tell the truth, I came here believing that you were the madman.

HENRY IV. (*suddenly indicating the Marchioness*). And she?

BELCREDI. Ah, as for her . . . I can't say. I see she is all fascinated by your words, by this *conscious* madness of yours. (*Turns to her*). Dressed as you are (*speaking to her*), you could even remain here to live it out, Marchioness.

DONNA MATILDA. You are insolent!

HENRY IV. (*conciliatingly*). No, Marchioness, what he means to say is that the miracle would be complete, according to him, with you here, who—as the Marchioness of Tuscany, you well know,—could not be my friend, save, as at Canossa, to give me a little pity . . .

BELCREDI. Or even more than a little! She said so herself!

HENRY IV. (*to the Marchioness, continuing*). And even, shall we say, a little remorse! . . .

BELCREDI. Yes, that too she has admitted.

DONNA MATILDA (*angry*). Now look here . . .

HENRY IV. (*quickly, to placate her*). Don't bother about him! Don't mind him! Let him go on infuriating me—

though the doctor's told him not to. (*Turns to Belcredi.*):
But do you suppose I am going to trouble myself any more
about what happened between us—the share you had in my
misfortune with her (*indicates the Marchioness to him and,
pointing Belcredi out to her*): the part he has now in
your life? This is my life! Quite a different thing from
your life! Your life, the life in which you have grown old
—I have not lived that life (*to Donna Matilda*). Was this
what you wanted to show me with this sacrifice of yours,
dressing yourself up like this, according to the Doctor's idea?
Excellently done, doctor! Oh, an excellent idea:—"As we
were then, eh? and as we are now?" But I am not a madman according to your way of thinking, doctor. I know
very well that that man there (*indicates Di Nolli*) cannot be
me; because I am Henry IV., and have been, these twenty
years, cast in this eternal masquerade. She has lived these
years (*indicates the Marchioness*)! She has enjoyed them
and has become—look at her!—a woman I can no longer
recognize. It is so that I knew her (*points to Frida and
draws near her*)! This is the Marchioness I know, always
this one! . . . You seem a lot of children to be so easily
frightened by me . . . (*To Frida*): And you're frightened
too, little girl, aren't you, by the jest that they made you
take part in—though they didn't understand it wouldn't be
the jest they meant it to be, for me? Oh miracle of miracles!
Prodigy of prodigies! The dream alive in you! More than
alive in you! It was an image that wavered there and
they've made you come to life! Oh, mine! You're mine,
mine, mine, in my own right! (*He holds her in his arms,
laughing like a madman, while all stand still terrified. Then
as they advance to tear Frida from his arms, he becomes
furious, terrible and cries imperiously to his valets*): Hold
them! Hold them! I order you to hold them!

(*The four young men amazed, yet fascinated, move to*

execute his orders, automatically, and seize Di Nolli, the doctor, and Belcredi.)

BELCREDI (*freeing himself*). Leave her alone! Leave her alone! You're no madman!

HENRY IV. (*In a flash draws the sword from the side of Landolph, who is close to him*). I'm not mad, eh! Take that, you! . . . (*Drives sword into him. A cry of horror goes up. All rush over to assist Belcredi, crying out together*):

DI NOLLI. Has he wounded you?

BERTHOLD. Yes, yes, seriously!

DOCTOR. I told you so!

FRIDA. Oh God, oh God!

DI NOLLI. Frida, come here!

DONNA MATILDA. He's mad, mad!

DI NOLLI. Hold him!

BELCREDI (*while they take him away by the left exit, he protests as he is borne out*). No, no, you're not mad! You're not mad. He's not mad!

(*They go out by the left amid cries and excitement. After a moment, one hears a still sharper, more piercing cry from Donna Matilda, and then, silence*).

HENRY IV. (*who has remained on the stage between Landolph, Harold and Ordulph, with his eyes almost starting out of his head, terrified by the life of his own masquerade which has driven him to crime*). Ah now . . . yes now . . . inevitably (*calls his valets around him as if to protect him*) here together . . . here together . . . for ever . . . for ever.

Curtain.

NOTE TO "HENRY IV."

With the author's consent and approval, the translator has omitted a few lines from the original Italian where their highly parenthetical character made the English version unnecessarily complex. One or two allusions have also been suppressed since they have not the same value in English as in Italian.—E. S.

RIGHT YOU ARE! (IF YOU THINK SO)
(*Così è, se vi pare!*)
A PARABLE IN THREE ACTS

BY

LUIGI PIRANDELLO

TRANSLATED BY

ARTHUR LIVINGSTON

CHARACTERS

LAMBERTO LAUDISI. SIGNORA FROLA. PONZA, SON-IN-LAW OF SIGNORA FROLA. SIGNORA PONZA, PONZA'S WIFE. COMMENDATORE AGAZZI, A PROVINCIAL COUNCILLOR. AMALIA, HIS WIFE. DINA, THEIR DAUGHTER. SIRELLI. SIGNORA SIRELLI, HIS WIFE. THE PREFECT. CENTURI, A POLICE COMMISSIONER. SIGNORA CINI. SIGNORA NENNI. A BUTLER. A NUMBER OF GENTLEMEN AND LADIES.

OUR OWN TIMES, IN A SMALL ITALIAN TOWN, THE CAPITAL OF A PROVINCE.

RIGHT YOU ARE! (IF YOU THINK SO)

ACT I

The parlor in the house of Commendatore Agazzi.
A door, the general entrance, at the back; doors leading to the wings, left and right.

LAUDISI *is a man nearing the forties, quick and energetic in his movements. He is smartly dressed, in good taste. At this moment he is wearing a semi-formal street suit: a sack coat, of a violet cast, with black lapels, and with black braid around the edges; trousers of a light but different color Laudisi has a keen, analytical mind, but is impatient and irritable in argument. Nevertheless, however angry he gets momentarily, his good humor soon comes to prevail. Then he laughs and lets people have their way, enjoying, meanwhile, the spectacle of the stupidity and gullibility of others.*

AMALIA, *Agazzi's wife, is Laudisi's sister. She is a woman of forty-five more or less. Her hair is already quite grey. Signora Agazzi is always showing a certain sense of her own importance from the position occupied by her husband in the community; but she gives you to understand that if she had a free rein she would be quite capable of playing her own part in the world and, perhaps, do it somewhat better than Commendatore Agazzi.*

DINA *is the daughter of Amalia and Agazzi. She is nineteen. Her general manner is that of a young person conscious of understanding everything better than papa and mamma; but this defect must not be exaggerated to the extent of con-*

cealing her attractiveness and charm as a good-looking winsome girl.

As the curtain rises Laudisi is walking briskly up and down the parlor to give vent to his irritation.

LAUDISI. I see, I see! So he did take the matter up with the prefect!

AMALIA. But Lamberto *dear,* please remember that the man is a subordinate of his.

LAUDISI. A subordinate of his . . . very well! But a subordinate in the office, not at home nor in society!

DINA. And he hired an apartment for that woman, his mother-in-law, right here in this very building, and on our floor.

LAUDISI. And why not, pray? He was looking for an apartment; the apartment was for rent, so he leased it—for his mother-in-law. You mean to say that a mother-in-law is in duty bound to make advances to the wife and daughter of the man who happens to be her son-in-law's superior on his job?

AMALIA. That is not the way it is, Lamberto. We didn't ask her to call on us. Dina and I took the first step by calling on her and—she *refused* to *receive* us!

LAUDISI. Well, is that any reason why your husband should go and lodge a complaint with the man's boss? Do you expect the government to order him to invite you to tea?

AMALIA. I think he deserves all he gets! That is not the way to treat two ladies. I hope he gets fired! The idea!

LAUDISI. Oh, you women! I say, making that complaint is a dirty trick. By Jove! If people see fit to keep to themselves in their own houses, haven't they a right to?

AMALIA. Yes, but you don't understand! We were trying to do her a favor. She is new in the town. We wanted to make her feel at home.

DINA. Now, now, Nunky dear, don't be so cross! Perhaps we did go there out of curiosity more than anything else; but it's all so funny, isn't it! Don't you think it was natural to feel just a little bit curious?

LAUDISI. Natural be damned! It was none of your business!

DINA. Now, see here, Nunky, let's suppose—here you are right here minding your own business and quite indifferent to what other people are doing all around you. Very well! I come into the room and right here on this table, under your very nose, and with a long face like an undertaker's, or, rather, with the long face of that jailbird you are defending, I set down—well, what?—anything—a pair of dirty old shoes!

LAUDISI. I don't see the connection.

DINA. Wait, don't interrupt me! I said a pair of old shoes. Well, no, not a pair of old shoes—a flat iron, a rolling pin, or your shaving brush for instance—and I walk out again without saying a word to anybody! Now I leave it to you, wouldn't you feel justified in wondering just a little, little, bit as to what in the world I meant by it?

LAUDISI. Oh, you're irresistible, Dina! And you're clever, aren't you? But you're talking with old Nunky, remember! You see, you have been putting all sorts of crazy things on the table here; and you did it with the idea of making me ask what it's all about; and, of course, since you were doing all that on purpose, you can't blame me if I do ask, why those old shoes just there, on that table, dearie? But what's all that got to do with it? You'll have to show me now that this Mr. Ponza of ours, that jail-bird as you say, or that rascal, that boor, as your father calls him, brought his mother-in-law to the apartment next to ours with the idea of stringing us all! You've got to show me that he did it on purpose!

DINA. I don't say that he did it on purpose—not at all! But you can't deny that this famous Mr. Ponza has come to this town and done a number of things which are unusual, to say the least; and which he must have known were likely to arouse a very natural curiosity in everybody. Look Nunky, here is a man: he comes to town to fill an important public position, and—what does he do? Where does he go to live? He hires an apartment on the *top* floor, if you please, of that dirty old tenement out there on the very outskirts of the town. Now, I ask you—did you ever see the place? Inside?

LAUDISI. I suppose you went and had a look at it?

DINA. Yes, Nunky dear, I went—with mamma! And we weren't the only ones, you know. The whole town has been to have a look at it. It's a five story tenement with an interior court so dark at noontime you can hardly see your hand before your face. Well, there is an iron balcony built out from the fifth story around the courtyard. A basket is hanging from the railing . . . They let it up and down—on a rope!

LAUDISI. Well, what of it?

DINA (*looking at him with astonished indignation*). What of it? Well, there, if you please, is where he keeps his wife!

AMALIA. While her mother lives here next door to us!

LAUDISI. A fashionable apartment, for his mother-in-law, in the residential district!

AMALIA. Generous to the old lady, eh? But he does that to keep her from seeing her daughter!

LAUDISI. How do you know that? How do you know that the old lady, rather, does not prefer this arrangement, just to have more elbow room for herself?

DINA. No, no, Nunky, you're wrong. Everybody knows that it is he who is doing it.

AMALIA. See here, Lamberto, everybody understands, if a girl, when she marries, goes away from her mother to live with her husband in some other town. But supposing this poor mother can't stand being separated from her daughter and follows her to the place, where she herself is also a complete stranger. And supposing now she not only does not live with her daughter, but is not even allowed to see her? I leave it to you . . . is that so easy to understand?

LAUDISI. Oh say, you have about as much imagination as so many mud turtles. A mother-in-law and a son-in-law! Is it so hard to suppose that either through her fault or his fault or the fault of both, they should find it hard to get along together and should therefore consider it wiser to live apart?

DINA (*with another look of pitying astonishment at her uncle*). How stupid of you, Nunky! The trouble is not between the mother-in-law and the son-in-law, but between the mother and the daughter.

LAUDISI. How do you know that?

DINA. Because he is as thick as pudding with the old lady; because they are always together, arm in arm, and as loving as can be. Mother-in-law and son-in-law, if you please! Whoever heard the like of that?

AMALIA. And he comes here every evening to see how the old lady is getting on!

DINA. And that is not the worst of it! Sometimes he comes during the daytime, once or twice!

LAUDISI. How scandalous! Do you think he is making love to the old woman?

DINA. Now don't be improper, uncle. No, we will acquit him of that. She is a poor old lady, quite on her last legs.

AMALIA. But he never, never, never brings his wife! A daughter kept from seeing her mother! The idea!

LAUDISI. Perhaps the young lady is not well; perhaps she isn't able to go out.

DINA. Nonsense! The old lady goes to see *her!*
AMALIA. Exactly! And she never gets in! She can see her only from a distance. Now will you explain to me why, in the name of common sense, that poor mother should be forbidden ever to enter her daughter's house?
DINA. And if she wants to talk to her she has to shout up from the courtyard!
AMALIA. Five stories, if you please! . . . And her daughter comes out and looks down from the balcony up there. The poor old woman goes into the courtyard and pulls a string that leads up to the balcony; a bell rings; the girl comes out and her mother talks up at her, her head thrown back, just as though she were shouting from out of a well. . . .

(*There is a knock at the door and the butler enters*).
BUTLER. Callers, madam!
AMALIA. Who is it, please?
BUTLER. Signor Sirelli, and the Signora with another lady, madam.
AMALIA. Very well, show them in.

(*The butler bows and withdraws*).

Sirelli, Signora Sirelli, Signora Cini appear in the doorway, rear.

SIRELLI, *also a man of about forty, is a bald, fat gentleman with some pretensions to stylish appearance that do not quite succeed: the overdressed provincial.*

SIGNORA SIRELLI, *his wife, plump, petite, a faded blonde, still young and girlishly pleasing. She, too, is somewhat overdressed with the provincial's fondness for display. She has the aggressive curiosity of the small-town gossip. She is chiefly occupied in keeping her husband in his place.*

SIGNORA CINI *is the old provincial lady of affected manners, who takes malicious delight in the failings of others, all the while affecting innocence and inexperience regarding the waywardness of mankind.*

AMALIA (*as the visitors enter, and taking Signora Sirelli's hands effusively*). Dearest! Dearest!

SIGNORA SIRELLI. I took the liberty of bringing my good friend, Signora Cini, along. She was so anxious to know you!

AMALIA. So good of you to come, Signora! Please make yourself at home! My daughter Dina, Signora Cini, and this is my brother, Lamberto Laudisi.

SIRELLI (*bowing to the ladies*). Signora, Signorina. (*He goes over and shakes hands with Laudisi.*)

SIGNORA SIRELLI. Amalia dearest, we have come here as to the fountain of knowledge. We are two pilgrims athirst for the truth!

AMALIA. The truth? Truth about what?

SIGNORA SIRELLI. Why . . . about this blessed Mr. Ponza of ours, the new secretary at the prefecture. He is the talk of the town, take my word for it, Amalia.

SIGNORA CINI. And we are all just dying to find out!

AMALIA. But we are as much in the dark as the rest of you, I assure you, madam.

SIRELLI (*to his wife*). What did I tell you? They know no more about it than I do. In fact, I think they know less about it than I do. Why is it this poor woman is not allowed to see her daughter? Do you know the reason, you people, the real reason?

AMALIA. Why, I was just discussing the matter with my brother.

LAUDISI. And my view of it is that you're all a pack of gossips!

DINA. The reason is, they say, that Ponza will not allow her to.

SIGNORA CINI. Not a sufficient reason, if I may say so, Signorina.

SIGNORA SIRELLI. Quite insufficient! There's more to it than that!

SIRELLI. I have a new item for you, fresh, right off the ice: he keeps her locked up at home!

AMALIA. His mother-in-law?

SIRELLI. No, no, his wife!

SIGNORA CINI. Under lock and key!

DINA. There, Nunky, what have you to say to that? And you've been trying to defend him all along!

SIRELLI (*staring in astonishment at Laudisi*). Trying to defend that man? Really . . .

LAUDISI. Defending him? No! I am not defending anybody. All I'm saying, if you ladies will excuse me, is that all this gossip is not worthy of you. More than that, you are just wasting your breath: because, so far as I can see, you're not getting anywhere at all.

SIRELLI. I don't follow you, sir!

LAUDISI. You're getting nowhere, my charming ladies!

SIGNORA CINI. But we're trying to get somewhere—we are trying to find out!

LAUDISI. Excuse me, what can you find out? What can we really know about other people—who they are—what they are—what they are doing, and why they are doing it?

SIGNORA SIRELLI. How can we know? Why not? By asking, of course! You tell me what you know, and I tell you what I know.

LAUDISI. In that case, madam, you ought to be the best informed person in the world. Why, your husband knows more about what others are doing than any other man—or woman, for that matter—in this neighborhood.

SIRELLI (*deprecatingly but pleased*). Oh I say, I say . . .

SIGNORA SIRELLI (*to her husband*). No dear, he's right,

he's right. (*Then turning to Amalia*): The real truth, Amalia, is this: for all my husband says he knows, I never manage to keep posted on anything!

SIRELLI. And no wonder! The trouble is—that woman never trusts me! The moment I tell her something she is convinced it is not *quite* as I say. Then, sooner or later, she claims that it *can't* be as I say. And at last she is certain it is the exact opposite of what I say!

SIGNORA SIRELLI. Well, you ought to hear all he tells me!

LAUDISI (*laughing aloud*). Hah! Hah! Hah! Hah! Hah! Hah! Hah! May I speak, madam? Let me answer your husband. My dear Sirelli, how do you expect your wife to be satisfied with things as you explain them to her, if you, as is natural, represent them as they seem to you?

SIGNORA SIRELLI. And that means—as they cannot possibly be!

LAUDISI. Why no, Signora, now you are wrong. From your husband's point of view things are, I assure you, exactly as he represents them.

SIRELLI. As they are in reality!

SIGNORA SIRELLI. Not at all! You are always wrong.

SIRELLI. No, not a bit of it! It is you who are always wrong. I am always right.

LAUDISI. The fact is that neither of you is wrong. May I explain? I will prove it to you. Now here you are, you, Sirelli, and Signora Sirelli, your wife, there; and here I am. You see me, don't you?

SIRELLI. Well . . . er . . . yes.

LAUDISI. Do you see me, or do you not?

SIRELLI. Oh, I'll bite! Of course I see you.

LAUDISI. So you see me! But that's not enough. Come here!

SIRELLI (*smiling, he obeys, but with a puzzled expression*

on his face as though he fails to understand what Laudisi is driving at). Well, here I am!

LAUDISI. Yes! Now take a better look at me . . . Touch me! That's it—that's it! Now you are touching me, are you not? And you see me! You're sure you see me?

SIRELLI. Why, I should say . . .

LAUDISI. Yes, but the point is, you're sure! Of course you're sure! Now if you please, Signora Sirelli, you come here—or rather . . . no . . . (*gallantly*) it is my place to come to you! (*He goes over to Signora Sirelli and kneels chivalrously on one knee*). You see me, do you not, madam? Now that hand of yours . . . touch me! A pretty hand, on my word! (*He pats her hand*).

SIRELLI. Easy! Easy!

LAUDISI. Never mind your husband, madam! Now, you have touched me, have you not? And you see me? And you are absolutely sure about me, are you not? Well now, madam, I beg of you; do not tell your husband, nor my sister, nor my niece, nor Signora Cini here, what you think of me; because, if you were to do that, they would all tell you that you are completely wrong. But, you see, you are really right; because I am really what you take me to be; though, my dear madam, that does not prevent me from also being really what your husband, my sister, my niece, and Signora Cini take me to be—because they also are absolutely right!

SIGNORA SIRELLI. In other words you are a different person for each of us.

LAUDISI. Of course I'm a different person! And you, madam, pretty as you are, aren't you a different person, too?

SIGNORA SIRELLI (*hastily*). No siree! I assure you, as far as I'm concerned, I'm always the same always, yesterday, today, and forever!

LAUDISI. Ah, but so am I, from my point of view, believe me! And, I would say that you are all mistaken unless you see me as I see myself; but that would be an inexcusable presumption on my part—as it would be on yours, my dear madam!

SIRELLI. And what has all this rigmarole got to do with it, may I ask?

LAUDISI. What has it got to do with it? Why . . . I find all you people here at your wits' ends trying to find out who and what other people are; just as though other people had to be this, or that, and nothing else.

SIGNORA SIRELLI. All you are saying is that we can never find out the truth! A dreadful idea!

SIGNORA CINI. I give up! I give up! If we can't believe even what we see with our eyes and feel with our fingers . . .

LAUDISI. But you must understand, madam! Of course you can believe what you see with *your* eyes and feel with *your* fingers. All I'm saying is that you should show some respect for what other people see with their eyes and feel with their fingers, even though it be the exact opposite of what you see and feel.

SIGNORA SIRELLI. The way to answer you is to refuse to talk with you. See, I turn my back on you! I am going to move my chair around and pretend you aren't in the room. Why, you're driving me crazy, crazy!

LAUDISI. Oh, I beg your pardon. Don't let me interfere with your party. Please go on! Pray continue your argument about Signora Frola and Signor Ponza—I promise not to interrupt again!

AMALIA. You're right for once, Lamberto; and I think it would be even better if you should go into the other room.

DINA. Serves you right, Nunky! Into the other room with you, into the other room!

LAUDISI. No, I refuse to budge! Fact is, I enjoy hearing

you gossip; but I promise not to say anything more, don't fear! At the very most, with your permission, I shall indulge in a laugh or two.

SIGNORA SIRELLI. How funny . . . and our idea in coming here was to find out . . . But really, Amalia, I thought this Ponza man was your husband's secretary at the Provincial building.

AMALIA. He is his secretary—in the office. But here at home what authority has Agazzi over the fellow?

SIGNORA SIRELLI. Of course! I understand! But may I ask . . . haven't you even tried to see Signora Frola, next door?

DINA. Tried? I should say we had! Twice, Signora!

SIGNORA CINI. Well . . . so then . . . you have probably talked to her . . .

DINA. We were not *received,* if you please!

SIGNORA SIRELLI, SIRELLI, SIGNORA CINI (*in chorus*). Not received? Why! Why! Why!

DINA. This very forenoon!

AMALIA. The first time we waited fully fifteen minutes at the door. We rang and rang and rang, and no one came. Why, we weren't even able to leave our cards! So we went back today . . .

DINA (*throwing up her hands in an expression of horror*). And *he* came to the door.

SIGNORA SIRELLI. Why yes, with that face of his . . . you can tell by just looking at the man . . . Such a face! Such a face! You can't blame people for talking! And then, with that black suit of his . . . Why, they all dress in black. Did you ever notice? Even the old lady! And the man's eyes, too! . . .

SIRELLI (*with a glance of pitying disgust at his wife*). What do you know about his eyes? You never saw his eyes! And you never saw the woman. How do you know she dresses in black? *Probably* she dresses in black . . . By the way, they come from a little town in the next county. Had you heard that? A village called Marsica!

AMALIA. Yes, the village that was destroyed a short time ago.

SIRELLI. Exactly! By an earthquake! Not a house left standing in the place.

DINA. And all their relatives were lost, I have heard. Not one of them left in the world!

SIGNORA CINI (*impatient to get on with the story*). Very well, very well, so then . . . he came to the door . . .

AMALIA. Yes . . . And the moment I saw him in front of me with that weird face of his I had hardly enough gumption left to tell him that we had just come to call on his mother-in-law, and he . . . well . . . not a word, not a word . . . not even a "thank you," if you please!

DINA. That is not quite fair, mama: . . . he did bow!

AMALIA. Well, yes, a bow . . . if you want to call it that. Something like this! . . .

DINA. And his eyes! You ought to see his eyes—the eyes of a devil, and then some! You never saw a man with eyes like that!

SIGNORA CINI. Very well, what did he say, finally?

DINA. He seemed quite taken aback.

AMALIA. He was all confused like; He hitched about for a time; and at last he said that Signora Frola was not feeling well, but that she would appreciate our kindness in having come; and then he just stood there, and stood there, apparently waiting for us to go away.

DINA. I never was more mortified in my life!

SIRELLI. A boor, a plain boor, I say! Oh, it's his fault, I am telling you. And . . . who knows? Perhaps he has got the old lady also under lock and key.

SIGNORA SIRELLI. Well, I think something should be

done about it! . . . After all, you are the wife of a superior of his. You can *refuse* to be treated like that.

AMALIA. As far as that goes, my husband did take it rather badly—as a lack of courtesy on the man's part; and he went straight to the prefect with the matter, insisting on an apology.

Signor Agazzi, commendatore and provincial councillor, appears in the doorway rear.

DINA. Oh goody, here's papa now!

AGAZZI *is well on toward fifty. He has the harsh, authoritarian manner of the provincial of importance. Red hair and beard, rather unkempt; gold-rimmed eyeglasses.*

AGAZZI. Oh Sirelli, glad to see you! (*He steps forward and bows to the company*).

AGAZZI. Signora! . . . (*He shakes hands with Signora Sirelli*).

AMALIA (*introducing Signora Cini*). My husband, Signora Cini!

AGAZZI (*with a bow and taking her hand*). A great pleasure, madam! (*Then turning to his wife and daughter in a mysterious voice*): I have come back from the office to give you some real news! Signora Frola will be here shortly.

SIGNORA SIRELLI (*clapping her hands delightedly*). Oh, the mother-in-law! She is coming? Really? Coming here?

SIRELLI (*going over to Agazzi and pressing his hand warmly as an expression of admiration*). That's the talk, old man, that's the talk! What's needed here is some show of authority.

AGAZZI. Why I had to, you see, I had to! . . . I can't let a man treat my wife and daughter that way! . . .

SIRELLI. I should say not! I was just expressing myself to that effect right here.

SIGNORA SIRELLI. And it would have been entirely proper to inform the prefect also . . .

AGAZZI (*anticipating*). . . . of all the talk that is going around on this fine gentleman's account? Oh, leave that to me! I didn't miss the opportunity.

SIRELLI. Fine! Fine!

SIGNORA CINI. And such talk!

AMALIA. For my part, I never heard of such a thing. Why, do you know, he has them both under lock and key!

DINA. No, mama, we are not *quite* sure of that. We are not *quite* sure about the old lady, yet.

AMALIA. Well, we know it about his wife, anyway.

SIRELLI. And what did the prefect have to say?

AGAZZI. Oh the prefect . . . well, the prefect . . . he was very much impressed, *very* much impressed, with what I had to say.

SIRELLI. I should hope so!

AGAZZI. You see, some of the talk had reached his ears already. And he agrees that it is better, as a matter of his own official prestige, for all this mystery in connection with one of his assistants to be cleared up, so that once and for all we shall know the truth.

LAUDISI. Hah, hah, hah, hah, hah, hah, hah!

AMALIA. That is Lamberto's usual contribution. He laughs!

AGAZZI. And what is there to laugh about?

SIGNORA SIRELLI. Why he says that no one can ever know the truth.

(*The butler appears at the door in back set*).

THE BUTLER. Excuse me, Signora Frola!

SIRELLI. Ah, here she is now!

AGAZZI. Now we'll see if we can settle it!

SIGNORA SIRELLI. Splendid! Oh, I am so glad I came.

AMALIA (*rising*). Shall we have her come in?

AGAZZI. Wait, you keep your seat, Amalia! Let's have

her come right in here. (*Turning to the butler*). Show her in!

Exit butler.

A moment later all rise as Signora Frola enters, and Amalia steps forward, holding out her hand in greeting.

SIGNORA FROLA *is a slight, modestly but neatly dressed old lady, very eager to talk and apparently fond of people. There is a world of sadness in her eyes, tempered however, by a gentle smile that is constantly playing about her lips.*

AMALIA. Come right in, Signora Frola! (*She takes the old lady's hand and begins the introductions*). Mrs. Sirelli, a good friend of mine; Signora Cini; my husband; Mr. Sirelli; and this is my daughter, Dina; my brother Lamberto Laudisi. Please take a chair, Signora!

SIGNORA FROLA. Oh, I am so very, very sorry! I have come to excuse myself for having been so negligent of my social duties. You, Signora Agazzi, were so kind, so very kind, to have honored me with a first call—when really it was my place to leave my card with you!

AMALIA. Oh, we are just neighbors, Signora Frola! Why stand on ceremony? I just thought that you, being new in town and all alone by yourself, would perhaps like to have a little company.

SIGNORA FROLA. Oh, how very kind of you it was!

SIGNORA SIRELLI. And you are quite alone, aren't you?

SIGNORA FROLA. Oh no! No! I have a daughter, married, though she hasn't been here very long, either.

SIRELLI. And your daughter's husband is the new secretary at the prefecture, Signor Ponza, I believe?

SIGNORA FROLA. Yes, yes, exactly! And I hope that Signor Agazzi, as his superior, will be good enough to excuse me—and him, too!

AGAZZI. I will be quite frank with you, madam! I was a bit put out.

SIGNORA FROLA (*interrupting*). And you were quite right! But I do hope you will forgive him. You see, we are still—what shall I say—still so upset by the terrible things that have happened to us . . .

AMALIA. You went through the earthquake, didn't you?

SIGNORA SIRELLI. And you lost all your relatives?

SIGNORA FROLA. Every one of them! All our family—yes, madam. And our village was left just a miserable ruin, a pile of bricks and stones and mortar.

SIRELLI. Yes, we heard about it.

SIGNORA FROLA. It wasn't so bad for me, I suppose. I had only one sister and her daughter, and my niece had no family. But my poor son-in-law had a much harder time of it. He lost his mother, two brothers, and their wives, a sister and her husband, and there were two little ones, his nephews.

SIRELLI. A massacre!

SIGNORA FROLA. Oh, one doesn't forget such things! You see, it sort of leaves you with your feet off the ground.

AMALIA. I can imagine.

SIGNORA SIRELLI. And all over-night with no warning at all! It's a wonder you didn't go mad.

SIGNORA FROLA. Well, you see, we haven't quite gotten our bearings yet; and we do things that may seem impolite, without in the least intending to. I hope you understand!

AGAZZI. Oh please, Signora Frola, of course!

AMALIA. In fact it was partly on account of your trouble that my daughter and I thought we ought to go to see you first.

SIGNORA SIRELLI (*literally writhing with curiosity*). Yes, of course, since they saw you all alone by yourself, and yet . . . excuse me, Signora Frola . . . if the question doesn't seem impertinent . . . how is it that when you have a daughter here in town and after a disaster like the one you have been through . . . I should think you people would all stand together, that you would need one another.

SIGNORA FROLA. Whereas I am left here all by myself?

SIRELLI. Yes, exactly. It does seem strange, to tell the honest truth.

SIGNORA FROLA. Oh, I understand—of course! But you know, I have a feeling that a young man and a young woman who have married should be left a good deal to themselves.

LAUDISI. Quite so, quite so! They should be left to themselves. They are beginning a life of their own, a life different from anything they have led before. One should not interfere in these relations between a husband and a wife!

SIGNORA SIRELLI. But there are limits to everything, Laudisi, if you will excuse me! And when it comes to shutting one's own mother out of one's life . . .

LAUDISI. Who is shutting her out of the girl's life? Here, if I have understood the lady, we see a mother who understands that her daughter cannot and must not remain so closely associated with her as she was before, for now the young woman must begin a new life on her own account.

SIGNORA FROLA (*with evidence of keen gratitude and relief*). You have hit the point exactly, sir. You have said what I would like to have said. You are exactly right! Thank you!

SIGNORA CINI. But your daughter, I imagine, often comes to see you . . .

SIGNORA FROLA (*hesitating, and manifestly ill at ease*). Why yes . . . I . . . I . . . we do see each other, of course!

SIRELLI (*quickly pressing the advantage*). But your daughter never goes out of her house! At least no one in town has ever seen her.

SIGNORA CINI. Oh, she probably has her little ones to take care of.

SIGNORA FROLA (*speaking up quickly*). No, there are no children yet, and perhaps there won't be any, now. You see, she has been married seven years. Oh, of course, she has a lot to do about the house; but that is not the reason, really. You know, we women who come from the little towns in the country—we are used to staying indoors much of the time.

AGAZZI. Even when your mothers are living in the same town, but not in your house? You prefer staying indoors to going and visiting your mothers?

AMALIA. But it's Signora Frola probably who visits her daughter.

SIGNORA FROLA (*quickly*). Of course, of course, why not! I go there once or twice a day.

SIRELLI. And once or twice a day you climb all those stairs up to the fifth story of that tenement, eh?

SIGNORA FROLA (*growing pale and trying to conceal under a laugh the torture of that cross-examination*). Why . . . er . . . to tell the truth, I don't go up. You're right, five flights would be quite too much for me. No, I don't go up. My daughter comes out on the balcony in the courtyard and . . . well . . . we see each other . . . and we talk!

SIGNORA SIRELLI. And that's all, eh? How terrible! You never see each other more intimately than that?

DINA. I have a mama and certainly I wouldn't expect her to go up five flights of stairs to see me, either; but at the same time I could never stand talking to her that way, shouting at the top of my lungs from a balcony on the fifth story. I am sure I should want a kiss from her occasionally, and feel her near me, at least.

SIGNORA FROLA (*with evident signs of embarrassment and confusion*). And you're right! Yes, exactly . . . quite right! I must explain. Yes . . . I hope you people are not going to think that my daughter is something she really is not. You must not suspect her of having so little regard for me and for my years, and you mustn't believe that I, her mother, am . . . well . . . five, six, even more stories to climb would never prevent a real mother, even if she were as old and infirm as I am, from going to her daughter's side and pressing her to her heart with a real mother's love . . . oh no!

SIGNORA SIRELLI (*triumphantly*). There you have it, there you have it, just as we were saying!

SIGNORA CINI. But there must be a reason, there must be a reason!

AMALIA (*pointedly to her brother*). Aha, Lamberto, now you see, there *is* a reason, after all!

SIRELLI (*insisting*). Your son-in-law, I suppose?

SIGNORA FROLA. Oh please, please, please, don't think badly of *him*. He is such a very good boy. Good is no name for it, my dear sir. You can't imagine all he does for me! Kind, attentive, solicitous for my comfort, everything! And as for my daughter—I doubt if any girl ever had a more affectionate and well-intentioned husband. No, on that point I am proud of myself! I could not have found a better man for her.

SIGNORA SIRELLI. Well then . . . What? What? *What?*

SIGNORA CINI. So your son-in-law is not the reason?

AGAZZI. I never thought it was his fault. Can you imagine a man forbidding his wife to call on her mother, or preventing the mother from paying an occasional visit to her daughter?

SIGNORA FROLA. Oh, it's not a case of forbidding! Who ever dreamed of such a thing! No, it's we, Commendatore, I and my daughter, that is. Oh, please, believe me! We refrain from visiting each other of our own accord, out of consideration for him, you understand.

AGAZZI. But excuse me . . . how in the world could he be offended by such a thing? I *don't* understand.

SIGNORA FROLA. Oh, please don't be angry, Signor Agazzi. You see it's a . . . what shall I say . . . a feeling . . . that's it, a feeling, which it would perhaps be very hard for anyone else to understand; and yet, when you do understand it, it's all so simple, I am sure . . . so simple . . . and believe me, my dear friends, it is no slight sacrifice that I am making, and that my daughter is making, too.

AGAZZI. Well, one thing you will admit, madam. This is a very, very unusual situation.

SIRELLI. Unusual, indeed! And such as to justify a curiosity even more persistent than ours.

AGAZZI. It is not only unusual, madam. I might even say it is suspicious.

SIGNORA FROLA. Suspicious? You mean you suspect Signor Ponza? Oh please, Commendatore, don't say that. What fault can you possibly find with him, Signor Agazzi?

AGAZZI. I didn't say just that . . . Please don't misunderstand! I said simply that the situation is so very strange that people might legitimately suspect . . .

SIGNORA FROLA. Oh, no, no, no! What could they suspect. We are in perfect agreement, all of us; and we are really quite happy, very happy, I might even say . . . both I and my daughter.

SIGNORA SIRELLI. Perhaps it's a case of jealousy?

SIGNORA FROLA. Jealousy of me? It would be hardly fair to say that, although . . . really . . . oh, it is so hard to explain! . . . You see, he is in love with my daughter . . . so much so that he wants her whole heart, her every thought, as it were, for himself; so much so that he insists that the affections which my daughter must have for me, her mother—he finds that love quite natural of course, why not? Of course he does!—should reach me through him—that's it, through him—don't you understand?

AGAZZI. Oh, that is going pretty strong! No, I don't understand. In fact it seems to me a case of downright cruelty!

SIGNORA FROLA. Cruelty? No, no, please don't call it cruelty, Commendatore. It is something else, believe me! You see it's so hard for me to explain the matter. Nature, perhaps ... but no, that's hardly the word. What shall I call it? Perhaps a sort of disease. It's a fullness of love, of a love shut off from the world. There, I guess that's it ... a fullness ... a completeness of devotion in which his wife must live without ever departing from it, and into which no other person must ever be allowed to enter.

DINA. Not even her mother, I suppose?

SIRELLI. It is the worst case of selfishness I ever heard of, if you want my opinion!

SIGNORA FROLA. Selfishness? Perhaps! But a selfishness, after all, which offers itself wholly in sacrifice. A case where the selfish person gives all he has in the world to the one he loves. Perhaps it would be fairer to call me selfish; for selfish it surely is for me to be always trying to break into this closed world of theirs, break in by force if necessary; when I know that my daughter is really so happy, so passionately adored— you ladies understand, don't you? A true mother should be satisfied when she knows her daughter is happy, oughtn't she? Besides I'm not completely separated from my daughter, am I? I see her and I speak to her (*She assumes a more confidential tone*). You see, when she lets down the basket there in the courtyard I always find a letter in it—a short note, which keeps me posted on the news of the day; and I put in a little letter that I have written. That is some consolation, a great consolation indeed, and now, in course of time, I've grown used to it. I am resigned, there! Resignation, that's it! And I've ceased really to suffer from it at all.

AMALIA. Oh well then, after all, if you people are satisfied, why should . . .

SIGNORA FROLA (*rising*). Oh yes, yes! But, remember, I told you he is such a good man! Believe me, he couldn't be better, really! We all have our weaknesses in this world, haven't we! And we get along best by having a little charity, a little indulgence, for one another. (*She holds out her hand to Amalia*). Thank you for calling, madam. (*She bows to Signora Sirelli, Signora Cini, and Dina; then turning to Agazzi, she continues*): And I do hope you have forgiven me!

AGAZZI. Oh, my dear madam, please, please! And we are extremely grateful for your having come to call on us.

SIGNORA FROLA (*offering her hand to Sirelli and Laudisi and again turning to Amalia who has risen to show her out*). Oh no, please, Signora Agazzi, please stay here with your friends! Don't put yourself to any trouble!

AMALIA. No, no, I will go with you; and believe me, we were very, very glad to see you!

(*Exit Signora Frola with Amalia showing her the way. Amalia returns immediately*).

SIRELLI. Well, there you have the story, ladies and gentlemen! Are you satisfied with the explanation?

AGAZZI. An explanation, you call it? So far as I can see she has explained nothing. I tell you there is some big mystery in all this business.

SIGNORA SIRELLI. That poor woman! Who knows what torment she must be suffering?

DINA. And to think of that poor girl!

SIGNORA CINI. She could hardly keep in her tears as she talked.

AMALIA. Yes, and did you notice when I mentioned all those stairs she would have to climb before really being able to see her daughter?

LAUDISI. What impressed me was her concern, which amounted to a steadfast determination, to protect her son-in-law from the slightest suspicion.

SIGNORA SIRELLI. Not at all, not at all! What could she say for him? She couldn't really find a single word to say for him.

SIRELLI. And I would like to know how anyone could condone such violence, such downright cruelty!

THE BUTLER (*appearing again in the doorway*). Beg pardon, sir! Signor Ponza calling.

SIGNORA SIRELLI. The man himself, upon my word!

(*An animated ripple of surprise and curiosity, not to say of guilty self-consciousness, sweeps over the company*).

AGAZZI. Did he ask to see me?

BUTLER. He asked simply if he might be received. That was all he said.

SIGNORA SIRELLI. Oh please, Signor Agazzi, please let him come in! I am really afraid of the man; but I confess the greatest curiosity to have a close look at the monster.

AMALIA. But what in the world can he be wanting?

AGAZZI. The way to find that out is to have him come in. (*To the butler*): Show him in, please.

(*The butler bows and goes out. A second later Ponza appears, aggressively, in the doorway*).

PONZA *is a short, thick set, dark complexioned man of a distinctly unprepossessing appearance; black hair, very thick and coming down low over his forehead; a black mustache upcurling at the ends, giving his face a certain ferocity of expression. He is dressed entirely in black. From time to time he draws a black-bordered handkerchief and wipes the perspiration from his brow. When he speaks his eyes are invariably hard, fixed, sinister.*

AGAZZI. This way please, Ponza, come right in! (*introducing him*): Signor Ponza, our new provincial secretary; my wife; Signora Sirelli; Signora Cini, my daughter Dina. This is Signor Sirelli; and here is Laudisi, my brother-in-law. Please join our party, won't you, Ponza?

PONZA. So kind of you! You will pardon the intrusion. I shall disturb you only a moment, I hope.

AGAZZI. You had some private business to discuss with me?

PONZA. Why yes, but I could discuss it right here. In fact, perhaps as many people as possible should hear what I have to say. You see it is a declaration that I owe, in a certain sense, to the general public.

AGAZZI. Oh my dear Ponza, if it is that little matter of your mother-in-law's not calling on us, it is quite all right; because you see . . .

PONZA. No, that was not what I came for, Commendatore. It was not to apologize for her. Indeed I may say that Signora Frola, my wife's mother, would certainly have left her cards with Signora Agazzi, your wife, and Signorina Agazzi, your daughter, long before they were so kind as to honor her with their call, had I not exerted myself to the utmost to prevent her coming, since I am absolutely unable to consent to her paying or receiving visits!

AGAZZI (*drawing up into an authoritative attitude and speaking with some severity*). Why? if you will be so kind as to explain, Ponza?

PONZA (*with evidences of increasing excitement in spite of his efforts to preserve his self-control*). I suppose my mother-in-law has been talking to you people about her daughter, my wife. Am I mistaken? And I imagine she told you further that I have forbidden her entering my house and seeing her daughter intimately.

AMALIA. Oh not at all, not at all, Signor Ponza! Signora Frola had only the nicest things to say about you. She could not have spoken of you with greater respect and kindness.

DINA. She seems to be very fond of you indeed.

AGAZZI. She says that she refrains from visiting your house of her own accord, out of regard for feelings of yours which we frankly confess we are unable to understand.

SIGNORA SIRELLI. Indeed, if we were to express our honest opinion . . .

AGAZZI. Well, yes, why not be honest? We think you are extremely harsh with the woman, extremely harsh, perhaps cruel would be an exacter word.

PONZA. Yes, that is what I thought; and I came here for the express purpose of clearing the matter up. The condition this poor woman is in is a pitiable one indeed—not less pitiable than my own perhaps; because, as you see, I am compelled to come here and make apologies—a public declaration—which only such violence as has just been used upon me could ever bring me to make in the world . . . (*He stops and looks about the room. Then he says slowly with emphatic emphasis on the important syllables*): My mother-in-law, Signora Frola, is not in her right mind! She is insane!

THE COMPANY. Insane! A lunatic! Oh my! Really! No! Impossible!

PONZA. And she has been insane for four years.

SIGNORA SIRELLI. Dear me, who would ever have suspected it! She doesn't show it in the least.

AGAZZI. Insane? Are you sure?

PONZA. She doesn't show it, does she? But she is insane, nevertheless; and her delusion consists precisely in believing that I am forbidding her to see her daughter. (*His face takes on an expression of cruel suffering mingled with a sort of ferocious excitement*). What daughter, for God's sake? Why her daughter died four years ago! (*A general sensation*).

EVERYONE AT ONCE. Died? She is dead? What do you mean? Oh, really? Four years ago? Why! Why!

PONZA. Four years ago! In fact it was the death of the poor girl that drove her mad.

SIRELLI. Are we to understand that the wife with whom you are now living . . .

PONZA. Exactly! She is my second wife. I married her two years ago.

AMALIA. And Signora Frola believes that her daughter is still living, that she is your wife still?

PONZA. Perhaps it was best for her that way. She was in charge of a nurse in her own room, you see. Well, when she chanced to see me passing by inadvertence on her street one day, with this woman, my second wife, she suddenly began to laugh and cry and tremble all over in an extreme of happiness. She was sure her daughter, whom she had believed dead, was alive and well; and from a condition of desperate despondency which was the first form of her mental disturbance, she entered on a second obsession, believing steadily that her daughter was not dead at all; but that I, the poor girl's husband, am so completely in love with her that I want her wholly for myself and will not allow anyone to approach her. She became otherwise quite well, you might say. Her nervousness disappeared. Her physical condition improved, and her powers of reasoning returned quite clear. Judge for yourself, ladies and gentlemen! You have seen her and talked with her. You would never suspect in the world that she is crazy.

AMALIA. Never in the world! Never!

SIGNORA SIRELLI. And the poor woman says she is so happy, so happy!

PONZA. That is what she says to everybody; and for that matter she really has a wealth of affection and gratitude for me; because, as you may well suppose, I do my very best, in spite of the sacrifices entailed, to keep up this benefical illusion in her. The sacrifices you can readily understand. In the first place I have to maintain two homes on my small salary. Then it is very hard on my wife, isn't it? But she, poor thing, does the very best she can to help me out! She comes to the window when the old lady appears. She talks to her from the balcony. She writes letters to her. But you people will understand that there are limits to what I can ask of my poor wife. Signora Frola, meanwhile, lives practically in confinement. We have to keep a pretty close watch on her. We have to lock her up, virtually. Otherwise, some fine day she would be walking right into my house. She is of a gentle, placid disposition fortunately; but you understand that my wife, good as she is, could never bring herself to accepting caresses intended for another woman, a dead woman! That would be a torment beyond conception.

AMALIA. Oh, of course! Poor woman! Just imagine!

SIGNORA SIRELLI. And the old lady herself consents to being locked up all the time?

PONZA. You, Commendatore, will understand that I couldn't permit her calling here except under absolute constraint.

AGAZZI. I understand perfectly, my dear Ponza, and you have my deepest sympathy.

PONZA. When a man has a misfortune like this fall upon him he must not go about in society; but of course when, by complaining to the prefect, you practically compelled me to have Signora Frola call, it was my duty to volunteer this further information; because, as a public official, and with due regard for the post of responsibility I occupy, I could not allow any discredible suspicions to remain attached to my reputation. I could not have you good people suppose for a moment that, out of jealousy or for any other reason, I could ever prevent a poor suffering mother from seeing her own daughter. (*He rises*). Again my apologies for having intruded my personal troubles upon your party. (*He bows*). My compliments, Commendatore. Good afternoon, good afternoon! Thank you! (*Bowing to Laudisi, Sirelli, and the others in turn, he goes out through the door, rear*).

AMALIA (*with a sigh of sympathy and astonishment*). Uhh! Crazy! What do you think of that?

SIGNORA SIRELLI. The poor old thing! But you wouldn't have believed it, would you?

DINA. I always knew there was something under it all.

SIGNORA CINI. But who could ever have guessed . . .

AGAZZI. Oh, I don't know, 1 don't know! You could tell from the way she talked . . .

LAUDISI. You mean to say that you thought . . . ?

AGAZZI. No, I can't say that. But at the same time, if you remember, she could never quite find her words.

SIGNORA SIRELLI. How could she, poor thing, out of her head like that?

SIRELLI. And yet, if I may raise the question, it seems strange to me that an insane person . . . oh, I admit that she couldn't really talk rationally . . . but what surprises me is her trying to find a reason to explain why her son-in-law should be keeping her away from her daughter. This effort of hers to justify it and then to adapt herself to excuses of her own invention . . .

AGAZZI. Yes, but that is only another proof that she's insane. You see, she kept offering excuses for Ponza that really were not excuses at all.

AMALIA. Yes, that's so. She would say a thing without really saying it, taking it back almost in the next words.

AGAZZI. But there is one more thing. If she weren't a downright lunatic, how could she or any other woman ever accept such a situation from a man? How could she ever consent to talk with her own daughter only by shouting up from the bottom of a well five stories deep?

SIRELLI. But if I remember rightly she has you there! Notice, she doesn't accept the situation. She says she is resigned to it. That's different! No, I tell you, there is still something funny about this business. What do you say, Laudisi?

LAUDISI. Why, I say nothing, nothing at all!

THE BUTLER (*appearing at the door and visibly excited*). Beg pardon, Signora Frola is here again!

AMALIA (*with a start*). Oh dear me, again? Do you suppose she'll be pestering us all the time now?

SIGNORA SIRELLI. I understand how you feel now that you know she's a lunatic.

SIGNORA CINI. My, my, what do you suppose she is going to say now?

SIRELLI. For my part I'd really like to hear what she's got to say.

DINA. Oh yes, mamma, don't be afraid! Ponza said she was quite harmless. Let's have her come in.

AGAZZAI. Of course, we can't send her away. Let's have her come in; and, if she makes any trouble, why . . . (*Turning to the butler*): Show her in. (*The butler bows and withdraws*).

AMALIA. You people stand by me, please! Why, I don't know what I am ever going to say to her now!

(*Signora Frola appears at the door. Amalia rises and steps forward to welcome her. The others look on in astonished silence*).

SIGNORA FROLA. May I please . . . ?
AMALIA. Do come in, Signora Frola, do come in! You know all these ladies. They were here when you came before.
SIGNORA FROLA (*with an expression of sadness on her features, but still smiling gently*). How you all look at me—and even you, Signora Agazzi! I am sure you think I am a lunatic, don't you!
AMALIA. My dear Signora Frola, what in the world are you talking about?
SIGNORA FROLA. But I am sure you will forgive me if I disturb you for a moment. (*Bitterly*): Oh, my dear Signora Agazzi, I wish I had left things as they were. It was hard to feel that I had been impolite to you by not answering the bell when you called that first time; but I could never have supposed that you would come back and force me to call upon you. I could foresee the consequences of such a visit from the very first.
AMALIA. Why, not at all, not at all! I don't understand. Why?
DINA. What consequences could you foresee, madam?
SIGNORA FROLA. Why, my son-in-law, Signor Ponza, has just been here, hasn't he?
AGAZZI. Why, yes, he was here! He came to discuss certain office matters with me . . . just ordinary business, you understand!
SIGNORA FROLA (*visibly hurt and quite dismayed*). Oh, I know you are saying that just to spare me, just in order not to hurt my feelings.
AGAZZI. Not at all, not at all! That was really why he came.
SIGNORA FROLA (*with some alarm*). But he was quite calm, I hope, quite calm?

AGAZZI. Calm? As calm as could be! Why not? Of course!

(*The members of the company all nod in confirmation*).

SIGNORA FROLA. Oh, my dear friends, I am sure you are trying to reassure me; but as a matter of fact I came to set you right about my son-in-law.

SIGNORA SIRELLI. Why no, Signora, what's the trouble?

AGAZZI. Really, it was just a matter of politics we talked about . . .

SIGNORA FROLA. But I can tell from the way you all look at me . . . Please excuse me, but it is not a question of me at all. From the way you all look at me I can tell that he came here to prove something that I would never have confessed for all the money in the world. You will all bear me out, won't you? When I came here a few moments ago you all asked me questions that were very cruel questions to me, as I hope you will understand. And they were questions that I couldn't answer very well; but anyhow I gave an explanation of our manner of living which can be satisfactory to nobody, I am well aware. But how could I give you the real reason? How could I tell you people, as he's doing, that my daughter has been dead for four years and that I'm a poor, insane mother who believes that her daughter is still living and that her husband will not allow me to see her?

AGAZZI (*quite upset by the ring of deep sincerity he finds in Signora Frola's manner of speaking*). What do you mean, your daughter?

SIGNORA FROLA (*hastily and with anguished dismay written on her features*). You know that's so. Why do you try to deny it? He did say that to you, didn't he?

SIRELLI (*with some hesitation and studying her features warily*). Yes . . . in fact . . . he did say that.

SIGNORA FROLA. I know he did; and I also know how

it pained him to be obliged to say such a thing of me. It is a great pity, Commendatore! We have made continual sacrifices, involving unheard of suffering, I assure you; and we could endure them only by living as we are living now. Unfortunately, as I well understand, it must look very strange to people, seem even scandalous, arouse no end of gossip! But after all, if he is an excellent secretary, scrupulously honest, attentive to his work, why should people complain? You have seen him in the office, haven't you? He is a good worker, isn't he?

AGAZZI. To tell the truth, I have not watched him particularly, as yet.

SIGNORA FROLA. Oh he really is, he really is! All the men he ever worked for say he's most reliable; and I beg of you, please don't let this other matter interfere. And why then should people go tormenting him with all this prying into his private life, laying bare once more a misfortune which he has succeeded in mastering and which, if it were widely talked about, might upset him again personally, and even hurt him in his career?

AGAZZI. Oh no, no, Signora, no one is trying to hurt him. It is nothing to his disgrace that I can see. Nor would we hurt you either.

SIGNORA FROLA. But my dear sir, how can you help hurting me when you force him to give almost publicly an explanation which is quite absurd—ridiculous I might even say! Surely people like you can't seriously believe what he says? You can't possibly be taking me for a lunatic? You don't really think that this woman is his second wife? And yet it is all so necessary! He needs to have it that way. It is the only way he can pull himself together; get down to his work again . . . the only way . . . the only way! Why he gets all wrought up, all excited, when he is forced to talk of this other matter; because he knows himself how hard it is for him to say certain things. You may have noticed it . . .

AGAZZI. Yes, that is quite true. He did seem very much excited.

SIGNORA SIRELLI. Well, well, well, so then it's he!

SIRELLI (*triumphantly*). I always said it was he.

AGAZZI. Oh, I say! Is that really possible? (*He motions to the company to be quiet*).

SIGNORA FROLA (*joining her hands beseechingly*). My dear friends, what are you really thinking? It is only on this subject that he is a little queer. The point is, you must simply not mention this particular matter to him. Why, really now, you could never suppose that I would leave my daughter shut up with him all alone like that? And yet, just watch him at his work and in the office. He does everything he is expected to do and no one in the world could do it better.

AGAZZI. But this is not enough, madam, as you will understand. Do you mean to say that Signor Ponza, your son-in-law, came here and made up a story out of whole cloth?

SIGNORA FROLA. Yes, sir, yes sir, exactly . . . only I will explain. You must understand—you must look at things from his point of view.

AGAZZI. What do you mean? Do you mean that your daughter is not dead?

SIGNORA FROLA. God forbid! Of course she is not dead!

AGAZZI. Well, then, he is the lunatic!

SIGNORA FROLA. No, no, look, look! . . .

SIRELLI. I always said it was he! . . .

SIGNORA FROLA. No, look, look, not that, not that! Let me explain . . . You have noticed him, haven't you? Fine, strong looking man. Well, when he married my daughter you can imagine how fond he was of her. But alas, she fell sick with a contagious disease; and the doctors had to separate her from him. Not only from him, of course, but from all her relatives. They're all dead now, poor things, in the earthquake, you understand. Well, he just refused to have her taken to the hospital; and he got so over-wrought that they actually had to put him under restraint; and he broke down nervously as the result of it all and he was sent to a sanatorium. But my daughter got better very soon, while he got worse and worse. He had a sort of obsession that his wife had died in the hospital, that perhaps they had killed her there; and you couldn't get that idea out of his head.

Just imagine when we brought my daughter back to him quite recovered from her illness—and a pretty thing she was to look at, too—he began to scream and say, no, no, no, she wasn't his wife, his wife was dead! He looked at her: No, no, no, not at all! She wasn't the woman! Imagine my dear friends, how terrible it all was. Finally he came up close to her and for a moment it seemed that he was going to recognize her again; but once more it was "No, no, no, she is not my wife!" And do you know, to get him to accept my daughter at all again, we were obliged to pretend having a second wedding, with the collusion of his doctors and his friends, you understand!

SIGNORA SIRELLI. Ah, so that is why he says that . . .

SIGNORA FROLA. Yes, but he doesn't really believe it, you know; and he hasn't for a long time, I am sure. But he seems to feel a need for maintaining the pretense. He can't do without it. He feels surer of himself that way. He is seized with a terrible fear, from time to time, that this little wife he loves may be taken from him again. (*Smiling and in a low, confidential tone*): So he keeps her locked up at home where he can have her all for himself. But he worships her—he worships her; and I am really quite convinced that my daughter is one of the happiest women in the world. (*She gets up*). And now I must be going. You see, my son-in-law is in a terrible state of mind at present. I wouldn't like to have him call, and find me not at home. (*With a sigh, and gesturing with her joined hands*): Well, I suppose we must get along as best we can; but it is hard on my poor girl. She has to pretend all along that she is not herself, but another, his second wife; and I . . . oh, as for me, I have to pretend that I am a lunatic when he's around, my dear friends; but I'm glad to, I'm glad to, really, so long as it does him some good. (*The ladies rise as she steps nearer to the door*). No, no, don't let me interrupt your party. I know the way out! Good afternoon! Good afternoon!

(*Bowing and smiling, she goes out through the rear door. The others stands there in silence, looking at each other with blank astonishment on their faces*).

LAUDISI (*coming forward*). So you want the truth, eh? The truth! The truth! Hah! hah! hah! hah! hah! hah! hah!

Curtain.

ACT II

Councillor Agazzi's study in the same house. Antique furnishings with old paintings on the walls. A portière over the rear entrance and over the door to the left which opens into the drawing room shown in the first act. To the right a substantial fireplace with a big mirror above the mantel. A flat top desk with a telephone. A sofa, armchairs, straight back chairs, etc.

As the curtain rises Agazzi is shown standing beside his desk with the telephone receiver pressed to his ear. Laudisi and Sirelli sit looking at him expectantly.

AGAZZI. Yes, I want Centuri. Hello . . . hello . . . Centuri? Yes, Agazzi speaking. That you, Centuri? It's me, Agazzi. Well? (*He listens for some time*). What's that? Really? (*Again he listens at length*). I understand, but you might go at the matter with a little more speed . . . (*Another long pause*). Well, I give up! How can that possibly be? (*A pause*). Oh, I see, I see . . . (*Another pause*). Well, never mind, I'll look into it myself. Goodbye, Centuri, goodbye! (*He lays down the receiver and steps forward on the stage*).

SIRELLI (*eagerly*). Well?
AGAZZI. Nothing! Absolutely nothing!
SIRELLI. Nothing at all?
AGAZZI. You see the whole blamed village was wiped out. Not a house left standing! In the collapse of the town hall, followed by a fire, all the records of the place seem to have been lost—births, deaths, marriages, everything.
SIRELLI. But not everybody was killed. They ought to be able to find somebody who knows them.

AGAZZI. Yes, but you see they didn't rebuild the place. Everybody moved away, and no record was ever kept of the people, of course. So far they have found nobody who knows the Ponzas. To be sure, if the police really went at it, they might find somebody; but it would be a tough job.

SIRELLI. So we can't get anywhere along that line! We have got to take what they say and let it go at that.

AGAZZI. That, unfortunately, is the situation.

LAUDISI (*rising*). Well, you fellows take a piece of advice from me: believe them both!

AGAZZI. What do you mean—"believe them both"? . . .

SIRELLI. But if she says one thing, and he says another . . .

LAUDISI. Well, in that case, you needn't believe either of them!

SIRELLI. Oh, you're just joking. We may not be able to verify the stories; but that doesn't prove that either one or the other may not be telling the truth. Some document or other . . .

LAUDISI. Oh, documents! Documents! Suppose you had them? What good would they do you?

AGAZZI. Oh, I say! Perhaps we can't get them now, but there were such documents once. If the old lady is the lunatic, there was, as there still may be somewhere, the death certificate of the daughter. Or look at it from the other angle: if we found all the records, and the death certificate were not there for the simple reason that it never existed, why then, it's Ponza, the son-in-law. He would be the lunatic.

SIRELLI. You mean to say you wouldn't give in if we stuck that certificate under your nose to-morrow or the next day? Would you still deny . . .

LAUDISI. Deny? Why . . . why . . . I'm not denying anything! In fact, I'm very careful not to be denying anything. You're the people who are looking up the records to be able to affirm or deny something. Personally, I don't give a rap for the documents; for the truth in my eyes is not a matter of black and white, but a matter of those two people. And into their minds I can penetrate only through what they say to me of themselves.

SIRELLI. Very well—She says he's crazy and he says she's crazy. Now one of them must be crazy. You can't get away from that. Well which is it, she or he?

AGAZZI. There, that's the way to put it!

LAUDISI. But just observe; in the first place, it isn't true that they are accusing each other of insanity. Ponza, to be sure, says his mother-in-law is insane. She denies this, not only of herself, but also of him. At the most, she says that he was a little off once, when they took her daughter from him; but that now he is quite all right.

SIRELLI. I see! So you're rather inclined, as I am, to trust what the old lady says.

AGAZZI. The fact is, indeed, that if you accept his story, all the facts in the case are explained.

LAUDISI. But all the facts in the case are explained if you take her story, aren't they?

SIRELLI. Oh, nonsense! In that case neither of them would be crazy! Why, one of them must be, damn it all!

LAUDISI. Well, which one? You can't tell, can you? Neither can anybody else! And it is not because those documents you are looking for have been destroyed in an accident —a fire, an earthquake—what you will; but because those people have concealed those documents in themselves, in their own souls. Can't you understand that? She has created for him, or he for her, a world of fancy which has all the earmarks of reality itself. And in this fictitious reality they get along perfectly well, and in full accord with each other; and this world of fancy, this reality of theirs, no document can possibly destroy because the air they breathe is of that world. For them it is something they can see with their eyes, hear with their ears, and touch with their fingers. Oh, I grant you—if you could get a death certificate or a marriage certificate or something of the kind, you might be able to satisfy that stupid curiosity of yours. Unfortunately, you can't get it. And the result is that you are in the extraordinary fix of having before you, on the one hand, a world of fancy, and on the other, a world of reality, and you, for the life of you, are not able to distinguish one from the other.

AGAZZI. Philosophy, my dear boy, philosophy! And I have no use for philosophy. Give me facts, if you please! Facts! So, I say, keep at it; and I'll bet you we get to the bottom of it sooner or later.

SIRELLI. First we got her story and then we got his; and then we got a new one from her. Let's bring the two of them together—and you think that then we won't be able to tell the false from the true?

LAUDISI. Well, bring them together if you want to! All I ask is permission to laugh when you're through.

AGAZZI. Well, we'll let you laugh all you want. In the meantime let's see . . . (*He steps to the door at the left and calls*): Amalia, Signora Sirelli, won't you come in here a moment?

(*The ladies enter with Dina*).

SIGNORA SIRELLLI (*catching sight of Laudisi and shaking a finger at him*). But how is it a man like you, in the presence of such an extraordinary situation, can escape the curiosity we all feel to get at the bottom of this mystery? Why, I lie awake nights thinking of it!

AGAZZI. As your husband says, that man's impossible! Don't bother about him, Signora Sirelli.

LAUDISI. No, don't bother with me; you just listen to Agazzi! He'll keep you from lying awake tonight.

AGAZZI. Look here, ladies. This is what I want—I have an idea: won't you just step across the hall to Signora Frola's?

AMALIA. But will she come to the door?

AGAZZI. Oh, I imagine she will!

DINA. We're just returning the call, you see . . .

AMALIA. But didn't he ask us not to call on his mother-in-law? Hasn't he forbidden her to receive visits?

SIRELLI. No, not exactly! That's how he explained what had happened; but at that time nothing was known. Now that the old lady, through force of circumstance, has spoken, giving her version at least of her strange conduct, I should think that . . .

SIGNORA SIRELLI. I have a feeling that she'll be awfully glad to see us, if for nothing else, for the chance of talking about her daughter.

DINA. And she really is a jolly old lady. There is no doubt in my mind, not the slightest: Ponza is the lunatic!

AGAZZI. Now, let's not go too fast. You just listen to me (*he looks at his wife*): don't stay too long—five or ten minutes at the outside!

SIRELLI (*to his wife*). And for heaven's sake, keep your mouth shut!

SIGNORA SIRELLI. And why such considerate advice to me?

SIRELLI. Once *you* get going . . .

DINA (*with the idea of preventing a scene*). Oh, we are not going to stay very long, ten minutes—fifteen, at the outside. I'll see that no breaks are made.

AGAZZI. And I'll just drop around to the office, and be back at eleven o'clock—ten or twenty minutes at the most.

SIRELLI. And what can I do?

AGAZZI. Wait! (*Turning to the ladies*). Now, here's

the plan! You people invent some excuse or other so as to get Signora Frola in here.

AMALIA. What? How can we possibly do that?

AGAZZI. Oh, find some excuse! You'll think of something in the course of your talk; and if you don't, there's Dina and Signora Sirelli. But when you come back, you understand, go into the drawing room. (*He steps to the door on the left, makes sure that it is wide open, and draws aside the portière*). This door must stay open, wide open, so that we can hear you talking from in here. Now, here are some papers that I ought to take with me to the office. However, I forget them here. It is a brief that requires Ponza's immediate personal attention. So then, I forget it. And when I get to the office I have to bring him back here to find them—See?

SIRELLI. But just a moment. Where do I come in? When am I expected to appear?

AGAZZI. Oh, yes! . . . A moment or two after eleven, when the ladies are again in the drawing room, and I am back here, you just drop in—to take your wife home, see? You ring the bell and ask for me, and I'll have you brought in here. Then I'll invite the whole crowd in! That's natural enough, isn't it?—into my office? . . .

LAUDISI (*interrupting*). And we'll have the Truth, the whole Truth with a capital T!

DINA. But look, Nunky, of course we'll have the truth —once we get them together face to face—capital T and all!

AGAZZI. Don't get into an argument with that man. Besides, it's time you ladies were going. None of us has any too much leeway.

SIGNORA SIRELLI. Come, Amalia, come Dina! And as for you, sir (*turning to Laudisi*), I won't even shake hands with you.

LAUDISI. Permit me to do it for you, madam. (*He shakes*

one hand with the other). Good luck to you, my dear ladies.

(*Exit Dina, Amalia, Signora Sirelli*).

AGAZZI (*to Sirelli*). And now we'd better go, too. Suppose we hurry!

SIRELLI. Yes, right away. Goodbye, Lamberto!

LAUDISI. Goodbye, good luck, good luck! (*Agazzi and Sirelli leave. Laudisi, left alone, walks up and down the study a number of times, nodding his head and occasionally smiling. Finally he draws up in front of the big mirror that is hanging over the mantelpiece. He sees himself in the glass, stops, and addresses his image*).

LAUDISI. So there you are! (*He bows to himself and salutes, touching his forehead with his fingers*). I say, old man, who is the lunatic, you or I? (*He levels a finger menacingly at his image in the glass; and, of course, the image in turn levels a finger at him. As he smiles, his image smiles*). Of course, I understand! I say it's you, and you say it's me. You—you are the lunatic! No? It's me? Very well! It's me! Have it *your* way. Between you and me, we get along very well, don't we! But the trouble is, others don't think of you just as I do; and that being the case, old man, what a fix you're in! As for me, I say that here, right in front of you, I can see myself with my eyes and touch myself with my fingers. But what are you for other people? What are you in their eyes? An image, my dear sir, just an image in the glass! "What fools these mortals be!" as old Shakespeare said. They're all carrying just such a phantom around inside themselves, and here they are racking their brains about the phantoms in other people; and they think all that is quite another thing!

(*The butler has entered the room in time to catch Laudisi gesticulating at himself in the glass. He wonders if the man is crazy. Finally he speaks up*):

BUTLER. Ahem! . . . Signor Laudisi, if you please . . .
LAUDISI (*coming to himself*). Uff!
BUTLER. Two ladies calling, sir! Signora Cini and another lady!
LAUDISI. Calling to see me?
BUTLER. Really, they asked for the signora; but I said that she was out—on a call next door; and then . . .
LAUDISI. Well, what then?
BUTLER. They looked at each other and said, "Really! Really!" and finally they asked me if anybody else was at home.
LAUDISI. And of course you said that everyone was out!
BUTLER. I said that you were in!
LAUDISI. Why, not at all! I'm miles and miles away! Perhaps that fellow they call Laudisi is here!
BUTLER. I don't understand, sir.
LAUDISI. Why? You think the Laudisi they know is the Laudisi I am?
BUTLER. I don't understand, sir.
LAUDISI. Whom are you talking to?
BUTLER. Who am I talking to? I thought I was talking to you.
LAUDISI. Are you really sure the Laudisi you are talking to is the Laudisi the ladies want to see?
BUTLER. Why, I think so, sir. They said they were looking for the brother of Signora Agazzi.
LAUDISI. Ah, in that case you are right! (*Turning to the image in the glass*): You are not the brother of Signora Agazzi? No, it's me! (*To the butler*): Right you are! Tell them I am in. And show them in here, won't you? (*The butler retires*).
SIGNORA CINI. May I come in
LAUDISI. Please, please, this way, madam!

SIGNORA CINI. I was told Signora Agazzi was not at home, and I brought Signora Nenni along. Signora Nenni is a friend of mine, and she was most anxious to make the acquaintance of . . .
LAUDISI. . . . of Signora Frola?
SIGNORA CINI. Of Signora Agazzi, your sister!
LAUDISI. Oh, she will be back very soon, and Signora Frola will be here, too.
SIGNORA CINI. Yes, we thought as much.

SIGNORA NENNI *is an oldish woman of the type of Signora Cini, but with the mannerisms of the latter somewhat more pronounced. She, too, is a bundle of concentrated curiosity, but of the sly, cautious type, ready to find something frightful under everything.*

LAUDISI. Well, it's all planned in advance! It will be a most interesting scene! The curtain rises at eleven, precisely!
SIGNORA CINI. Planned in advance? What is planned in advance?
LAUDISI (*mysteriously, first with a gesture of his finger and then aloud*). Why, bringing the two of them together! (*A gesture of admiration*): Great idea, I tell you!
SIGNORA CINI. The two of them—together—who?
LAUDISI. Why, the two of them. He—in here! (*Pointing to the room about him*).
SIGNORA CINI. Ponza, you mean?
LAUDISI. And she—in there! (*He points toward the drawing room*).
SIGNORA CINI. Signora Frola?
LAUDISI. Exactly! (*With an expressive gesture of his hands and even more mysteriously*): But afterwards, all of them—in here! Oh, a great idea, a great idea!
SIGNORA CINI. In order to get . . .
LAUDISI. The truth! Precisely: the truth!
SIGNORA CINI. But the truth is known already!

LAUDISI. Of course! The only question is stripping it bare, so that everyone can see it!

SIGNORA CINI (*with the greatest surprise*). Oh, really? So they know the truth! And which is it—He or she?

LAUDISI. Well, I'll tell you . . . you just guess! Who do you think it is?

SIGNORA CINI (*ahemming*). Well . . . I say . . . really . . . you see . . .

LAUDISI. Is it she or is it he? You don't mean to say you don't know! Come now, give a guess!

SIGNORA CINI. Why, for my part I should say . . . well, I'd say . . . . it's *he*.

LAUDISI (*looks at her admiringly*). Right you are! It *is* he!

SIGNORA CINI. Really? I always thought so! Of course, it was perfectly plain all along. It had to be he!

SIGNORA NENNI. All of us women in town said it was he. We always said so!

SIGNORA CINI. But how did you get at it? I suppose Signor Agazzi ran down the documents, didn't he—the birth certificate, or something?

SIGNORA NENNI. Through the prefect, of course! There was no getting away from those people. Once the police start investigating . . . !

LAUDISI (*motions to them to come closer to him; then in a low voice and in the same mysterious manner, and stressing each syllable*). The certificate!—Of the second marriage!

SIGNORA CINI (*starting back with astonishment*). What?

SIGNORA NENNI (*likewise taken aback*). What did you say? The second marriage?

SIGNORA CINI. Well, in that case he was *right*.

LAUDISI. Oh, documents, ladies, documents! This certificate of the second marriage, so it seems, talks as plain as day.

Signora Nenni. Well, then, *she* is the lunatic.
Laudisi. Right you are! She it is!
Signora Cini. But I thought you said . . .
Laudisi. Yes, I did say . . . but this certificate of the second marriage may very well be, as Signora Frola said, a fictitious document, gotten up through the influence of Ponza's doctors and friends to pamper him in the notion that his wife was not his first wife, but another woman.
Signora Cini. But it's a public document. You mean to say a public document can be a fraud?
Laudisi. I mean to say—well, it has just the value that each of you chooses to give it. For instance, one could find somewhere, possibly, those letters that Signora Frola said she gets from her daughter, who lets them down in the basket in the courtyard. There are such letters, aren't there?
Signora Cini. Yes, of course!
Laudisi. They are documents, aren't they? Aren't letters documents? But it all depends on how you read them. Here comes Ponza, and he says they are just made up to pamper his mother-in-law in her obsession . . .
Signora Cini. Oh, dear, dear, so then we're never sure about anything?
Laudisi. Never sure about anything? Why not at all, not at all! Let's be exact. We are sure of many things, aren't we? How many days are there in the week? Seven—Sunday, Monday, Tuesday, Wednesday . . . How many months in the year are there? Twelve: January, February, March . . .
Signora Cini. Oh, I see, you're just joking! You're just joking! (*Dina appears, breathless, in the doorway, at the rear*).
Dina. Oh, Nunky, won't you please . . . (*She stops at the sight of Signora Cini*). Oh, Signora Cini, you here?
Signora Cini. Why, I just came to make a call! . . .

LAUDISI. . . . with Signora Cenni.

SIGNORA NENNI. No, my name is Nenni.

LAUDISI. Oh yes, pardon me! She was anxious to make Signora Frola's acquaintance . . .

SIGNORA NENNI. Why, not at all!

SIGNORA CINI. He has just been making fun of us! You ought to see what fools he made of us!

DINA. Oh, he's perfectly insufferable, even with mamma and me. Will you excuse me for just a moment? No, everything is all right. I'll just run back and tell mamma that you people are here and I think that will be enough. Oh, Nunky, if you had only heard her talk! Why, she is a perfect *dear,* and what a good, kind soul! . . . She showed us all those letters her daughter wrote . . .

SIGNORA CINI. Yes, but as Signor Laudisi was just saying . . .

DINA. He hasn't even seen them!

SIGNORA NENNI. You mean they are not really fictitious?

DINA. Fictitious nothing! They talk as plain as day. And such things! You can't fool a mother when her own daughter talks to her. And you know—the letter she got yesterday! . . . (*She stops at the sound of voices coming into the study from the drawing room*). Oh, here they are, here they are, already! (*She goes to the door and peeps into the room*).

SIGNORA CINI (*following her to the door*). Is *she* there, too?

DINA. Yes, but you had better come into the other room. All of us women must be in the drawing room. And it is just eleven o'clock, Nunky!

AMALIA (*entering with decision from the door on the left*). I think this whole business is quite unnecessary! We have absolutely no further need of proofs . . .

DINA. Quite so! I thought of that myself. Why bring Ponza here?

AMALIA (*taken somewhat aback by Signora Cini's presence*). Oh, my dear Signora Cini! ...

SIGNORA CINI (*introducing Signora Nenni*). A friend of mine, Signora Nenni! I ventured to bring her with me ...

AMALIA (*bowing, but somewhat coolly, to the visitor*). A great pleasure, Signora! (*After a pause*). There is not the slightest doubt in the world: ... it's he!

SIGNORA CINI. It's he? Are you sure it's he?

DINA. And such a trick on the poor old lady!

AMALIA. Trick is not the name for it! It is downright dishonest!

LAUDISI. Oh, I agree with you: it's outrageous! Quite! So much so, I'm quite convinced it must be *she!*

AMALIA. She? What do you mean? How can you say that?

LAUDISI. I say, it is *she,* it is *she,* it's *she!*

AMALIA. Oh, I say! If you had heard her talk ... !

DINA. It is absolutely clear to us now.

SIGNORA CINI and SIGNORA NENNI (*swallowing*). Really? You are sure?

LAUDISI. Exactly! Now that you are sure it's he, why, obviously—it must be she.

DINA. Oh dear me, why talk to that man? He is just impossible!

AMALIA. Well, we must go into the other room ... This way, if you please!

(*Signora Cini, Signora Nenni and Amalia withdraw through the door on the left. Dina starts to follow, when Laudisi calls her back*).

LAUDISI. Dina!

DINA. I refuse to listen to you! I refuse!

LAUDISI. I was going to suggest that, since the whole matter is closed, you might close the door also.

DINA. But papa . . . he told us to leave it open. Ponza will be here soon; and if papa finds it closed—well, you know how papa is!

LAUDISI. But you can convince him! . . . You especially. You can show him that there really was no need of going any further. You are convinced yourself, aren't you?

DINA. I am as sure of it, as I am that I'm alive!

LAUDISI (*putting her to the test with a smile*). Well, close the door then!

DINA. I see, you're trying to make me say that I'm not really sure. Well, I won't close the door, but it's just on account of papa.

LAUDISI. Shall I close it for you?

DINA. If you take the responsibility yourself! . . .

LAUDISI. But you see, *I* am sure! I *know* that Ponza is the lunatic!

DINA. The thing for you to do is to come into the other room and just hear her talk a while. Then you'll be sure, absolutely sure. Coming?

LAUDISI. Yes, I'm coming, and I'll close the door behind me—on my own responsibility, of course.

DINA. Ah, I see. So you're convinced even before you hear her talk.

LAUDISI. No, dear, it's because I'm sure that your papa, who has been with Ponza, is just as certain as you are that any further investigation is unnecessary.

DINA. How can you say that?

LAUDISI. Why, of course, if you talk with Ponza, you're sure the old lady is crazy. (*He walks resolutely to the door*). I am going to shut this door.

DINA (*restraining him nervously, then hesitating a mo-*

ment). Well, why not . . . if you're really sure? What do you say—let's leave it open!

LAUDISI. Hah! hah! hah! hah! hah! hah! hah!

DINA. But just because papa told us to!

LAUDISI. And papa will tell you something else by and by. Say . . . let's leave it open!

(*A piano starts playing in the adjoining room—an ancient tune, full of soft and solemn melody; the "Nina" of Pergolesi*).

DINA. Oh, there she is. She's playing! Do you hear? Actually playing the piano!

LAUDISI. The old lady?

DINA. Yes! And you know? She told us that her daughter used to play this tune, always the same tune. How well she plays! Come! Come!

(*They hurry through the door*).

The stage, after the exit of Laudisi and Dina, remains empty for a space of time while the music continues from the other room. Ponza, appearing at the door with Agazzi, catches the concluding notes and his face changes to an expression of deep emotion—an emotion that will develop into a virtual frenzy as the scene proceeds.

AGAZZI (*in the doorway*). After you, after you, please! (*He takes Ponza's elbow and motions him into the room. He goes over to his desk, looks about for the papers which he pretends he had forgotten, finds them eventually and says*). Why, here they are! I was sure I had left them here. Won't you take a chair, Ponza? (*Ponza seems not to hear. He stands looking excitedly at the door into the drawing room, through which the sound of the piano is still coming*).

AGAZZI. Yes, they are the ones! (*He takes the papers*

and steps to Ponza's side, opening the fold). It is an old case, you see. Been running now for years and years! To tell you the truth I haven't made head or tail of the stuff myself. I imagine you'll find it one big mess. (*He, too, becomes aware of the music and seems somewhat irritated by it. His eyes also rest on the door to the drawing room*). That noise, just at this moment! (*He walks with a show of anger to the door*). Who is that at the piano anyway? (*In the doorway he stops and looks, and an expression of astonishment comes into his face*). Ah!

PONZA (*going to the door also. On looking into the next room he can hardly restrain his emotion*). In the name of God, is *she* playing?

AGAZZI. Yes—Signora Frola! And how well she does play!

PONZA. How is this? You people have brought her in here, again! And you're letting her play!

AGAZZI. Why not? What's the harm?

PONZA. Oh, please, please, no, not that song! It is the one her daughter used to play.

AGAZZI. Ah, I see! And it hurts you?

PONZA. Oh, no, not me—but her—it hurts her—and you don't know how much! I thought I had made you and those women understand just how that poor old lady was!

AGAZZI. Yes, you did . . . quite true! But you see . . . but see here, Ponza! (*trying to pacify the man's growing emotion*).

PONZA (*continuing*). But you *must* leave her alone! You *must* not go to her house! She *must* not come in here! I am the only person who can deal with her. You are killing her . . . killing her!

AGAZZI. No, I don't think so. It is not so bad as that. My wife and daughter are surely tactful enough . . . (*Suddenly the music ceases. There is a burst of applause*).

AGAZZI. There, you see. Listen! Listen!

(*From the next room the following conversation is distinctly heard*).

DINA. Why, Signora Frola, you are perfectly *marvellous* at the piano!

SIGNORA FROLA. But you should hear how my Lena plays!

(*Ponza digs his nails into his hands*).

AGAZZI. Her daughter, of course!

PONZA. Didn't you hear? "How my Lena plays! How my Lena *plays*"!

(*Again from the inside*).

SIGNORA FROLA. Oh, no, not now! . . . She hasn't played for a long time—since that happened. And you know, it is what she takes hardest, poor girl!

AGAZZI. Why, that seems quite natural to me! Of course, she thinks the girl is still alive!

PONZA. But she shouldn't be allowed to say such things. She *must* not—she *must* not say such things! Didn't you hear? "She hasn't played since that happened"! She said "she *hasn't* played since that happened"! Talking of the piano, you understand! Oh, you don't understand, no, of course! My first wife had a piano and played that tune. Oh, oh, oh! You people are determined to ruin me!

(*Sirelli appears at the back door at this moment, and hearing the concluding words of Ponza and noticing his extreme exasperation, stops short, uncertain as to what to do. Agazzi is himself very much affected and motions to Sirelli to come in*).

AGAZZI. Why, no, my dear fellow, I don't see any reason . . . (*To Sirelli*). Won't you just tell the ladies to come in here?

(*Sirelli, keeping at a safe distance from Ponza, goes to the door at the left and calls*).

PONZA. The ladies in here? In here with me? Oh, no, no, please, rather . . .

(*At a signal from Sirelli, who stands in the doorway to the left, his face taut with intense emotion, the ladies enter. They all show various kinds and degrees of excitement and emotion. Signora Frola appears, and catching sight of Ponza in the condition he is in, stops, quite overwhelmed. As he assails her during the lines that follow, she exchanges glances of understanding from time to time with the ladies about her. The action here is rapid, nervous, tense with excitement, and extremely violent*).

PONZA. You? Here? How is this? You! Here! Again! What are you doing here?

SIGNORA FROLA. Why, I just came . . . don't be cross!

PONZA. You came here to tell these ladies . . . What did you tell these ladies?

SIGNORA FROLA. Nothing! I swear to God, nothing!

PONZA. Nothing? What do you mean, nothing? I heard you with my own ears, and this gentleman here heard you also. You said "she plays". Who plays? Lena plays! And you know very well that Lena has been dead for four years. Dead, do you hear! Your daughter has been dead —for four years!

SIGNORA FROLA. Yes, yes, I know . . . Don't get excited, my dear . . . Oh, yes, oh yes. I know . . .

PONZA. And you said "she hasn't been able to play since that happened". Of course she hasn't been able to play since that happened. How could she, if she's dead?

SIGNORA FROLA. Why, of course, certainly. Isn't that what I said? Ask these ladies. I said that she hasn't been able to play since that happened. Of course. How could she, if she's dead?

PONZA. And why were you worrying about that piano, then?

Signora Frola. No, no! I'm not worrying about any piano . . .

Ponza. I broke that piano up and destroyed it. You know that, the moment your daughter died, to keep this second wife of mine from playing on it. For that matter you know that this second woman never plays.

Signora Frola. Why, of course, dear! Of course! She doesn't know how to play!

Ponza. And one thing more: Your daughter was Lena, wasn't she? Her name was Lena. Now, see yere! You just tell these people what my second wife's name is. Speak up! You know very well what her name is! What is it? What is it?

Signora Frola. Her name is Julia! Yes, yes, of course, my dear friends, her name is Julia! (*Winks at someone in the company*).

Ponza. Exactly! Her name is Julia, and not Lena! Who are you winking at? Don't you go trying to suggest by those winks of yours that she's not Julia!

Signora Frola. Why, what do you mean? I wasn't winking! Of course I wasn't!

Ponza. I saw you! I saw you very distinctly! You are trying to ruin me! You are trying to make these people think that I am keeping your daughter all to myself, just as though she were not dead. (*He breaks into convulsive sobbing*) . . . just as though she were not dead!

Signora Frola (*hurrying forward and speaking with infinite kindness and sympathy*). Oh no! Come, come, my poor boy. Come! Don't take it so hard. I never said any such thing, did I, madam!

Amalia, Signora Sirelli, Dina. Of course she never said such a thing! She always said the girl was dead! Yes! Of course! No!

Signora Frola. I did, didn't I? I said she's dead,

didn't I? And that you are so very good to me. Didn't I, didn't I? I, trying to ruin you? I, trying to get you into trouble?

PONZA. And you, going into other people's houses where there are pianos, playing your daughter's tunes on them! Saying that Lena plays them that way, or even better!

SIGNORA FROLA. No, it was . . . why . . . you see . . . it was . . . well . . . just to see whether . . .

PONZA. But you *can't* . . . you *mustn't!* How could you ever dream of trying to play a tune that your dead daughter played!

SIGNORA FROLA. You are quite right! . . . Oh, yes! Poor boy! Poor boy! (*She also begins to weep*). I'll never do it again: Never, never, never again!

PONZA (*advancing upon her threateningly*). What are you doing here? Get out of here! Go home at once! Home! Home! Go home!

SIGNORA FROLA. Yes, Yes! Home! I am going home! Oh dear, oh dear!

(*She backs out the rear door, looking beseechingly at the company, as though urging everyone to have pity on her son-in-law. She retires, sobbing. The others stand there looking at Ponza with pity and terror; but the moment Signora Frola has left the room, he regains his normal composure, an air of despairing melancholy, and he says coolly, but with profound seriousness*):

PONZA. I hope you good people will excuse me for this scene. A scene it really was, I suppose! But how could I avoid it? I had to rave like that to repair the damage which you good people, with the best of intentions, and surely without dreaming what you are really doing, have done to this unfortunate woman.

AGAZZI (*in astonishment*). What do you mean? That you were just acting? You were pretending all that?

PONZA. Of course I was! Don't you people understand that I had to? The only way to keep her in her obsession is for me to shout the truth that way, as though I myself had gone mad, as though I were the lunatic! Understand? But please forgive me. I must be going now. I must go in and see how she is. (*He hurries out through the rear door. The others stand where they are in blank amazement*).

LAUDISI (*coming forward*). And there, ladies and gentlemen, you have the truth! Hah! hah! hah; hah; hah; hah! hah!

Curtain.

ACT III

The same scene. As the curtain rises, Laudisi is sprawling in an easy chair, reading a book. Through the door that leads into the parlor on the left comes the confused murmur of many voices.

The butler appears in the rear door, introducing the police commissioner, CENTURI. CENTURI *is a tall, stiff, scowling official, with a decidedly professional air. He is in the neighborhood of forty.*

THE BUTLER. This way, sir. I will call Signor Agazzi at once.

LAUDISI (*drawing himself up in his chair and looking around*). Oh, it's you, Commissioner! (*He rises hastily and recalls the butler, who has stepped out through the door*). One moment, please! Wait! (*To Centuri*). Anything new, Commissioner?

COMMISSIONER (*stiffly*). Yes, something new!

LAUDISI. Ah! Very well. (*To the butler*): Never mind. I'll call him myself. (*He motions with his hand toward the door on the left. The butler bows and withdraws*).

You have worked miracles, Commissioner! You're the savior of this town. Listen! Do you hear them! You are the lion of the place! How does it feel to be the father of your country? But say, what you've discovered is all solid fact?

COMMISSIONER. We've managed to unearth a few people.

LAUDISI. From Ponza's town? People who know all about him?

[Act III] RIGHT YOU ARE! 209

COMMISSIONER. Yes! And we have gathered from them a few facts,—not many, perhaps, but well authenticated.

LAUDISI. Ah, that's nice. Congratulations! For example . . .

COMMISSISONER. For example? Why, for instance, here . . . well, here are all the communications I have received. Read 'em yourself!

(*From an inner pocket he draws a yellow envelope, opened at one end, from which he takes a document and hands it to Laudisi*).

LAUDISI. Interesting, I am sure. Very interesting! ..

(*He stands, reading the document carefully, commenting from time to time with exclamations in different tones. First an "ah" of satisfaction, then another "ah" which attenuates this enthusiasm very much. Finally an "eh" of disappointment, which leads to another "eh" of complete disgust*). Why, no, what's all this amount to, Commissioner?

COMMISSIONER. Well, it's what we were able to find out.

LAUDISI. But this doesn't prove anything, you understand! It leaves everything just where it was. There's nothing of any significance whatever here. (*He looks at the commissioner for a moment and then, as though suddenly making up his mind, he says*): I wonder, Commissioner, would you like to do something really great—render a really distinguished service to this town; and meanwhile lay up a treasure in heaven?

COMMISSIONER (*looking at him in perplexity*). What are you thinking of sir?

LAUDISI. I'll explain. Here, please, take this chair! (*He sets the chair in front of Agazzi's desk*). I advise you, Mr. Commissioner, to tear up this sheet of paper that you've brought and which has absolutely no significance at all. But here on this other piece of paper, why don't you write down something that will be precise and clear?

COMMISSIONER. Why . . . why . . . myself? What do you mean? What should I write?

LAUDISI. Anything, anything at all! Anything that comes into your head, provided, however, it be *precise* and *clear!* Say, for instance, that Signora Frola is a lunatic, or, if you will, if you prefer, that the second marriage of Ponza's was a frame-up!

COMMISSIONER. I don't get you, Signor Laudisi. What are you driving at? I forge the document?

LAUDISI (*insisting*). Forge? Just say something—anything—that these two old acquaintances of Ponza's whom you managed to get hold of might have said. Come, Commissioner, rise to the occasion! Do something for the commonwealth! Bring this town back to normal again! Don't you see what they are after? They all want the truth—*a* truth, that is: Something specific; something concrete! They don't care what it is. All they want is something categorical, something that speaks plainly! Then they'll quiet down.

COMMISSIONER. *The* truth—*a* truth? Excuse me, have I understood you clearly? You were suggesting that I commit a forgery? I am astonished that you dare propose such a thing, and when I say I am astonished, I'm not saying half what I actually feel. Be so good as to tell the Commendatore that I am here!

LAUDISI (*dropping his arms dejectedly*). As you will, Commissioner!

(*He steps over to the door on the left. As he draws the portières and swings the door more widely open, the voices become louder and more confused. As he steps through, there is a sudden silence. The police commissioner stands waiting with a satisfied air, twirling one of the points of his mustache. All of a sudden, there is commotion and cheer-*

ing in the next room. Cries of delight and applause, mixed with hand-clapping. The police commissioner comes out of his reverie and looks up with an expression of surprise on his features, as though not understanding what it's all about. Through the door to the left come Agazzi, Sirelli, Laudisi, Amalia, Dina, Signora Sirelli, Signora Cini, Signora Nenni, and many other ladies and gentlemen. Agazzi leads the procession. They are all still talking and laughing excitedly, clapping their hands, and crying "I told you so! Fine! Fine! Good! How wonderful! Now we'll know!" etc.).

AGAZZI (*stepping forward cordially*). Ah, my dear Centuri, I was sure you could! Nothing ever gets by *our* chief!

COMPANY. Fine! Good! What did you find out! Have you brought something? Is it she? Is it he? Tell us?

COMMISSIONER (*who doesn't yet understand what all the excitement is about. For him it has been a mere matter of routine*). Why, no . . . why, Commendatore, simply . . . you understand . . .

AGAZZI. Hush! Give him a chance! . . .

COMMISSIONER. I have done my best. I . . . but what did Signor Laudisi tell you?

AGAZZI. He told us that you have brought news, real news!

SIRELLI. Specific data, clear, precise! . . .

LAUDISI (*amplifying*). . . . not many, perhaps, but well authenticated! The best they've managed to trace! Old neighbors of Ponza, you see; people well acquainted with him . . .

EVERYBODY. Ah! At last! At last! Now we'll know! At last!

(*The Commissioner hands the document to Agazzi*).

COMMISSIONER. There you have it, Commendatore!

AGAZZI (*opening the sheet, as all crowd around him*). Let's have a look at it!
COMMISSIONER. But you, Signor Laudisi . . .
LAUDISI. Don't interrupt, please, the document speaks for itself! Agazzi, you read it.
AGAZZI (*to Laudisi*). But give me a chance, won't you? Please! Please! Now! There you are!
LAUDISI. Oh, I don't care. I've read the thing already.
EVERYBODY (*crowding around him*). You've read it already? What did it say? Is it he? Is it she?
LAUDISI (*speaking very formally*). There is no doubt whatever, as a former neighbor of Ponza's testifies, that the woman Frola was once in a sanatorium!
THE GROUP (*cries of disappointment*). Oh really! Too bad! Too bad!
SIGNORA SIRELLI. Signora Frola, did you say?
DINA. Are you sure it was she?
AGAZZI. Why, no! Why, no, it doesn't say anything of the kind! (*Coming forward and waving the document triumphantly*). It doesn't say anything of the kind! (*General excitement*).
EVERYBODY. Well, what does it say? What does it say?
LAUDISI (*insisting*). It does too! It says "the Frola woman"—the Frola woman, categorically.
AGAZZI. Nothing of the kind! The witness says that he *thinks* she was in a sanatorium. He does not assert that she was. Besides, there is another point. He doesn't know whether this Frola woman who was in a sanatorium was the mother or the daughter, the first wife, that is!
EVERYBODY (*with relief*). Ah!
LAUDISI (*insistingly*). But I say he does. It must be the mother! Who else could it be
SIRELLI. No, of course, it's the daughter! It's the daughter!

SIGNORA SIRELLI. Just as the old lady said herself!

AMALIA. Exactly! That time when they took her away by force from her husband! . . .

DINA. Yes, she says that her daughter was taken to a sanatorium on account of a contagious disease.

AGAZZI. Furthermore, observe another thing. The witness does not really belong to their town. He says that he used to go there frequently, but that he does not remember particularly. He remembers that he heard something or other! . . .

SIRELLI. Ah! How can you depend on such a man's testimony? Nothing but hearsay!

LAUDISI. But, excuse me! If all you people are so sure that Signora Frola is right, what more do you want? Why do you go looking for documents? This is all nonsense!

SIRELLI. If it weren't for the fact that the prefect has accepted Ponza's side of the story, I'll tell you . . .

COMMISSIONER. Yes, that's true. The prefect said as much to me . . .

AGAZZI. Yes, but that's because the prefect has never talked with the old lady who lives next door.

SIGNORA SIRELLI. You bet he hasn't. He talked only with Ponza.

SIRELLI. But, for that matter, there are other people of the same mind as the prefect.

A GENTLEMAN. That is my situation, my situation exactly. Yes sir! Because I know of just such as case where a mother went insane over the death of her daughter and insists that the daughter's husband will not allow her to see the girl. The same case to a *T*.

A SECOND GENTLEMAN. Not exactly to a T! Not exactly to a T! In the case you mention the man didn't marry again. Here, this man Ponza is living with another woman . . .

LAUDISI (*his face brightening with a new idea that has suddenly come to him*). I have it, ladies and gentlemen! Did you hear that? It's perfectly simple. Dear me, as simple as Columbus's egg!

EVERYBODY. What? What? What? What?

THE SECOND GENTLEMAN. What did I say? I didn't realize it was important.

LAUDISI. Just a moment, ladies and gentlemen! (*Turning to Agazzi*): Is the prefect coming here, by chance?

AGAZZI. Yes, we were expecting him. But what's the new idea?

LAUDISI. Why, you were bringing him here to talk with Signora Frola. So far, he is standing by Ponza. When he has talked with the old lady, he'll know whether to believe Ponza or her. That's *your* idea! Well, I've thought of something better that the prefect can do. Something that he only can do.

EVERYBODY. What is it? What is it? What is it?

LAUDISI (*triumphantly*). Why, this wife of Ponza's, of course . . . at least, the woman he is living with! What this gentleman said suggested the idea to me.

SIRELLI. Get the second woman to talk? Of course! Of course!

DINA. But how can we, when she is kept under lock and key?

LAUDISI. Why, the prefect can use his authority—order her to speak!

AMALIA. Certainly, she is the one who can clear up the whole mystery.

SIGNORA SIRELLI. I don't believe it. She'll say just what her husband tells her to say.

LAUDISI. Of course, if she were to speak in his presence . . . of course!

SIRELLI. She must speak with the prefect privately, all by himself.

AGAZZI. And the prefect, as the final authority over the man, will insist that the wife make a formal explicit statement before him. Of course, of course! What do you say, Commissioner?

COMMISSIONER. Why certainly, there's no doubt that if the prefect were so inclined . . .

AGAZZI. It is the only way out of it, after all. We ought to 'phone him and explain that he needn't go to the trouble of coming here. You attend to that, will you, Commissioner?

COMMISSIONER. Very glad to! My compliments, ladies! Good afternoon, gentlemen!

SIGNORA SIRELLI. A good idea for once, Laudisi.

DINA. Oh, Nunky, how clever of you! Wise old Nunky!

THE COMPANY. The only way out of it! Yes! Yes! Fine! At last!

AGAZZI. Curious none of us thought of that before!

SIRELLI. Not so curious! None of us ever set eyes on the woman. She might as well be in another world, poor girl.

LAUDISI (*as though suddenly impressed by this latter reflection*). In another world? Why yes,—are you really sure there is such a woman?

AMALIA. Oh I say! Please, please, Lamberto!

SIRELLI (*with a laugh*). You mean to say you think there is no such woman?

LAUDISI. How can you be sure there is? You can't guarantee it!

DINA. But the old lady sees her and talks with her every day.

SIGNORA SIRELLI. And Ponza says that, too. They both agree on that point!

LAUDISI. Yes, yes, I don't deny that. But just a moment! If you think of it, isn't Signora Frola right? Well, in that case who is the woman in Ponza's eyes? The phantom of a second wife, of course! Or else Ponza himself is right, and in that case you have the phantom of a daughter in the old lady's eyes! Two phantoms, in other words! Now we've got to find out, ladies and gentlemen, whether this woman, who must be a mere phantom for the one or for the other, is a person, after all for herself. In the situation we are in, I should say there was very good ground for doubting.

AGAZZI. Oh, you make me tired! If we listen to you . . .

LAUDISI. No, ladies and gentlemen, notice! It may be that she is nothing but a phantom in her own eyes.

SIGNORA NENNI. Why, this is getting to be almost spooky!

SIGNORA CINI. You mean to say it's a ghost, a real ghost? How can you frighten us so?

EVERYBODY. Nonsense! He's only joking! He's only joking!

LAUDISI. Not a bit of it! I'm not joking at all! Who ever saw the woman? No one ever set eyes on her. He talks of her, to be sure; and she, the old woman that is, says that she often sees her.

SIRELLI. Nonsense! Any number of people have seen her; she comes to the balcony of the courtyard.

LAUDISI. Who comes to the balcony?

SIRELLI. A woman in flesh and bones—in skirts, for that

matter. People have seen her and people have heard her talk. For heaven's sake, man!

LAUDISI. Are you sure of that?

AGAZZI. And why not, pray? You said so yourself a moment ago!

LAUDISI. Why yes, I did say so! I did say that the prefect ought to have a talk with whatever woman is there. But notice one thing, it is certain that no ordinary woman is there. No *ordinary* woman! Of that much we can be sure! And I, for my part, have come to doubt whether she is in any sense of the term, a woman.

SIGNORA SIRELLI Dear me, dear me! That man simply drives me crazy.

LAUDISI. Well, supposing we wait and see!

EVERYBODY. Well, who is she then? But people have seen her! His wife! On the balcony! She writes letters!

POLICE COMMISSIONER (*in the heat of the confusion comes into the room, excitedly announcing*). The prefect is coming! The prefect!

AGAZZI. What do you mean? Coming here? But you went to . . .

COMMISSIONER. Why yes, but I met him hardly a block away. He was coming here; and Ponza is with him.

SIRELLI. Ah, Ponza!

AGAZZI. Oh, if Ponza is with him, I doubt whether he is coming here. They are probably on their way to the old lady's. Please, Centuri, you just wait on the landing there and ask him if he won't step in here as he promised?

COMMISSIONER. Very well! I'll do so! (*He withdraws hurriedly through the door in the rear*).

AGAZZI. Won't you people just step into the other room?

SIGNORA SIRELLI. But remember now, be sure to make him see the point! It's the only way out, the only way.

AMALIA (*at the door to the left*). This way, ladies, if you please!

AGAZZI. Won't you just stay here, Sirelli; and you, too, Lamberto?

(*All the others go out through the door to the left*).

AGAZZI (*to Laudisi*). But let me do the talking, won't you!

LAUDISI. Oh, as for that, don't worry. In fact, if you prefer, I'll go into the other room . . .

AGAZZI. No, no, it's better for you to be here. Ah, here he is now!

THE PREFECT *is a man of about sixty, tall, thick set, good natured, affable.*

PREFECT. Ah, Agazzi, glad to see you. How goes it, Sirelli? Good to see you again, Laudisi. (*He shakes hands all around*).

AGAZZI (*motioning toward a chair*). I hope you won't mind my having asked you to come here.

PREFECT. No, I was coming, just as I promised you!

AGAZZI (*noticing the police commissioner at the door*). Oh, I'm sorry, Commissioner! Please come in! Here, have a chair!

PREFECT (*good-naturedly to Sirelli*). By the way, Sirelli, they tell me that you've gone half nutty over this blessed affair of our new secretary.

SIRELLI. Oh, no, governor, believe me. I'm not the only one! The whole village is worked up.

AGAZZI. And that's putting it very mildly.

PREFECT. What's it all about? What's it all about? Good heavens!

AGAZZI. Of course, governor, you're probably not posted

[Act III]   *RIGHT YOU ARE!*   219

on the whole business. The old lady lives here next door. . . .

PREFECT. Yes, I understand so.

SIRELLI. No, one moment, please, governor. You haven't talked with the poor old lady yet.

PREFECT. I was on my way to see her. (*Turning to Agazzi*). I had promised you to see her here, but Ponza came and begged me, almost on my knees, to see her in her own house. His idea was to put an end to all this talk that's going around. Do you think he would have done such a thing if he weren't absolutely sure?

AGAZZI. Of course, he's sure! Because when she's talking in front of him, the poor woman . . .

SIRELLI (*suddenly getting in his oar*). She says just what he wants her to say, governor; which proves that she is far from being as insane as he claims.

AGAZZI. We had a sample of that, here, yesterday, all of us.

PREFECT. Why, I understand so. You see he's trying all the time to make her believe he's crazy. He warned me of that. And how else could he keep the poor woman in her illusion? Do you see any way? All this talk of yours is simply torture to the poor fellow! Believe me, pure torture!

SIRELLI. Very well, governor! But supposing *she* is the one who is trying to keep *him* in the idea that her daughter is dead; so as to reassure him that his wife will not be taken from him again. In that case, you see, governor, it's the old lady who is being tortured, and not Ponza!

AGAZZI. The moment you see the possibility of that, governor . . . Well, you ought to hear her talk; but all by herself, when he's not around. Then you'd see the possibility all right . . .

SIRELLI. Just as we all see it!

PREFECT. Oh, I wonder! You don't seem to me so awfully sure; and for my part, I'm quite willing to confess that I'm not so sure myself. How about you, Laudisi?

LAUDISI. Sorry, governor, I promised Agazzi here to keep my mouth shut.

AGAZZI (*protesting angrily*). Nothing of the kind! How dare you say that? When the governor asks you a plain question . . . It's true I told him not to talk, but do you know why? He's been doing his best for the past two days to keep us all rattled so that we can't find out anything.

LAUDISI. Don't you believe him, governor. On the contrary. I've been doing my best to bring these people to common sense.

SIRELLI. Common sense! And do you know what he calls common sense? According to him it is not possible to discover the truth; and now he's been suggesting that Ponza is living not with a woman, but with a ghost!

PREFECT (*enjoying the situation*). That's a new one! Quite an idea! How do you make that out, Laudisi?

AGAZZI. Oh, I say! . . . You know how he is. There's no getting anywhere with him!

LAUDISI. I leave it to you, governor. I was the one who first suggested bringing the woman here.

PREFECT. And do you think, Laudisi, I ought to see the old lady next door?

LAUDISI. No, I advise no such thing, governor. In my judgment you are doing very well in depending on what Ponza tells you.

PREFECT. Ah, I see! Because you, too, think that Ponza . . .

LAUDISI. No, not at all . . . because I'm also satisfied to have all these people stand on what Signora Frola says, if that does them any good.

[ACT III] *RIGHT YOU ARE!* 221

AGAZZI. So you see, eh, governor? That's what you call arguing, eh?

PREFECT. Just a moment! Let me understand! (*Turning to Laudisi*): So you say we can also trust what the old lady says?

LAUDISI. Of course you can! Implicitly! And so you can depend upon what Ponza says. Implicitly!

PREFECT. Excuse me, I don't follow you!

SIRELLI. But man alive, if they both say the exact opposite of each other! . . .

AGAZZI (*angrily and with heat*). Listen to me, governor, please. I am prejudiced neither in favor of the old lady nor in favor of Ponza. I recognize that he may be right and that she may be right. But we ought to settle the matter, and there is only one way to do it.

SIRELLI. The way that Laudisi here suggested.

PREFECT. He suggested it? That's interesting? What is it?

AGAZZI. Since we haven't been able to get any positive proof, there is only one thing left. You, as Ponza's final superior, as the man who can fire him if need be, can obtain a statement from his wife.

PREFECT. Make his wife talk, you mean?

SIRELLI. But not in the presence of her husband, you understand.

AGAZZI. Yes, making sure she tells the truth!

SIRELLI. . . . tell whether she's the daughter of Signora Frola, that is, as we think she must be . . .

AGAZZI. . . . or a second wife who is consenting to impersonate the daughter of Signora Frola, as Ponza claims.

PREFECT. . . . and as I believe myself, without a shadow of doubt! (*Thinking a moment*), Why, I don't see any objection to having her talk. Who could object? Ponza? But Ponza, as I know very well, is more eager than anybody else to have this talk quieted down. He's all upset over this whole business, and said he was willing to do anything I proposed. I'm sure he will raise no objection. So if it will ease the minds of you people here . . . Say, Centuri (*the police commissioner rises*), won't you just ask Ponza to step in here a moment? He's next door with his mother-in-law.

COMMISSIONER. At once, Your Excellency! (*He bows and withdraws through the door at the rear*).

AGAZZI. Oh well, if he consents . . .

PREFECT. He'll consent, all right. And we'll be through with it in a jiffy. We'll bring her right in here so that you people . . .

AGAZZI. Here, in my house?

SIRELLI. You think he'll let his wife come in here?

PREFECT. Just leave it to me, just leave it to me! I prefer to have her right here because, otherwise you see, you people would always suppose that I and Ponza had . . .

AGAZZI. Oh, please, governor, no! That's not fair!

SIRELLI. Oh, no, governor, we trust you implicitly!

PREFECT. Oh, I'm not offended, not at all! But you know very well that I'm on his side in this matter; and you'd always be thinking that to hush up any possible scandal in connection with a man in my office . . . No, you see. I must insist on having the interview here . . . Where's your wife, Agazzi?

AGAZZI. In the other room, governor, with some other ladies.

PREFECT. Other ladies? Aha, I see! (*Laughing*). You have a regular detective bureau here, eh? (*The police commissioner enters with Ponza*).

COMMISSIONER. May I come in? Signor Ponza is here.

PREFECT. Thanks, Centuri. This way, Ponza, come right in! (*Ponza bows*).

AGAZZI. Have a chair, Ponza. (*Ponza bows and sits down*).

PREFECT. I believe you know these gentlemen? (*Ponza rises and bows*).

AGAZZI. Yes, I introduced them yesterday. And this is Laudisi, my wife's brother. (*Ponza bows*).

PREFECT. I venture to disturb you, my dear Ponza, just to tell you that here with these friends of mine . . . (*At the first words of the prefect, Ponza evinces the greatest nervousness and agitation*).

PREFECT. Was there something you wanted to say, Ponza?

PONZA. Yes, there is something I want to say, governor. I want to present my resignation here and now.

PREFECT. Oh, my dear fellow, I'm so sorry! But just a few moments ago down at the office you were talking . . .

PONZA. Oh, really, this is an outrage, governor! This is just plain persecution, plain persecution!

PREFECT. Oh, now, don't take it that way, old man. See here. These good people . . .

AGAZZI. Persecution, did you say? On my part? . . .

PONZA. On the part of all of you! And I am sick and tired of it! I am going to resign, governor. I refuse to submit to this ferocious prying into my private affairs which will end by undoing a work of love that has cost me untold sacrifice these past two years. You don't know, governor! Why, I've treated that dear old lady in there just as tenderly as though she were my own mother. And yesterday I had to shout at her in the most cruel and terrible way! Why, I found her just now so worked up and excited that . . .

AGAZZI. That's queer! While she was in here Signora Frola was quite mistress of herself. If anybody was worked up, Ponza, it was you. And even now, if I might say . . .

PONZA. But you people don't know what you're making me go through!

PREFECT. Oh, come, come, my dear fellows, don't take it so hard. After all, I'm here, am I not? And you know I've always stood by you! And I always will!

PONZA. Yes, governor, and I appreciate your kindness, really!

PREFECT. And then you say that you're as fond of this poor old lady as you would be if she were your own mother. Well, now, just remember that these good people here seem to be prying into your affairs because they, too, are fond of her! . . .

PONZA. But they're killing her, I tell you, governor! They're killing her, and I warned them in advance.

PREFECT. Very well, Ponza, very well! Now we'll get through with this matter in no time. See here, it is all very simple. There is one way that you can convince these people without the least doubt in the world. Oh, not me—I don't need convincing. I believe *you*.

PONZA. But *they* won't believe me, no matter what I say.

AGAZZI. That's not so! When you came here after your mother-in-law's first visit and told us that she was insane, all of us . . . well, we were surprised, but we believed you. (*Turning to the prefect*): But after he left, you understand, the old lady came back . . .

PREFECT. Yes, yes, I know. He told me. (*Turning to Ponza again*). She came back here and said that she was trying to do with you exactly what you say you were trying to do with her. It's natural, isn't it, that people hearing both stories, should be somewhat confused. Now you see that these good people, in view of what your mother-in-law says, can't possibly be sure of what you say. So there you are. Now, such being the case, you and your mother-in-law—

why, it's perfectly simple—you two just step aside. Now you know you're telling the truth, don't you? So do I! So you can't possibly object to their hearing the testimony of the only person who does know, aside from you two.

PONZA. And who may that be, pray?

PREFECT. Why, your wife!

PONZA. My wife! (*Decisively and angrily*). Ah, no! I refuse! Never in the world! Never!

PREFECT. And why not, old man?

PONZA. Bring my wife here to satisfy the curiosity of these strangers?

PREFECT (*sharply*). And my curiosity, too, if you don't mind! What objection can you have?

PONZA. Oh, but governor, no! My wife! Here? No! Why drag my wife in? These people ought to believe me!

PREFECT. But don't you see, my dear fellow, that the course you're taking now is just calculated to discredit what you say?

AGAZZI. His mistake in the first place, governor, was trying to prevent his mother-in-law from coming here and calling—a double discourtesy, mark you, to my wife and to my daughter!

PONZA. But what in the name of God do you people want of me? You've been nagging and nagging at that poor old woman next door; and now you want to get your clutches on my wife! No, governor! I refuse to submit to such an indignity! She owes nothing to anybody. My wife is not making visits in this town. You say you believe me, governor? That's enough for me! Here's my resignation! I'll go out and look for another job!

PREFECT. No, no, Ponza, I must speak plainly. In the first place I have always treated you on the square; and you have no right to speak in that tone of voice to me. In the second place you are beginning to make me doubt your word by refusing to furnish me—not other people—but me, the evidence that I have asked for in your interest, evidence, moreover, that so far as I can see, cannot possibly do you any harm. It seems to me that my colleague here, Signor Agazzi, can ask a lady to come to his house! But no, if you prefer, we'll go and see her.

PONZA. So you really insist, governor?

PREFECT. I insist, but as I told you, in your own interest. You realize, besides, that I might have the legal right to question her . . .

PONZA. I see, I see! So that's it! An official investigation! Well, why not, after all? I will bring my wife here, just to end the whole matter. But how can you guarantee me that this poor old lady next door will not catch sight of her?

PREFECT. Why, I hadn't thought of that! She does live right next door.

AGAZZI (*speaking up*). We are perfectly willing to go to Signor Ponza's house.

PONZA. No, no, I was just thinking of you people. I don't want you to play any more tricks on me. Any mistakes might have the most frightful consequences, set her going again!

AGAZZI. You're not very fair to us, Ponza, it seems to me.

PREFECT. Or you might bring your wife to my office, rather . . .

PONZA. No, no! Since you're going to question her anyway, we might as well get through with it. We'll bring her here, right here. I'll keep an eye on my mother-in-law myself. We'll have her here right away, governor, and get an end of this nonsense once and for all, once and for all! (*He hurries away through the rear exit.*)

PREFECT. I confess I was not expecting so much opposition on his part.

AGAZZI. Ah, you'll see. He'll go and cook up with his wife just what she's to say!

PREFECT. Oh, don't worry as to that! I'll question the woman myself.

SIRELLI. But he's more excited than he's ever been before.

PREFECT. Well, I confess I never saw him just in this state of mind. Perhaps it is the sense of outrage he feels in having to bring his wife . . .

SIRELLI. In having to let her loose for once, you ought to say!

PREFECT. A man isn't necessarily crazy because he wants to keep an eye on his wife.

AGAZZI. Of course he says it's to protect her from the mother-in-law.

PREFECT. I wasn't thinking of just that—he may be jealous of the woman!

SIRELLI. Jealous to the extent of refusing her a servant? For you know, don't you, he makes his wife do all the housework?

AGAZZI. And he does all the marketing himself every morning.

COMMISSIONER. That's right, governor! I've had him shadowed. An errand boy from the market carries the stuff as far as the door.

SIRELLI. But he never lets the boy inside.

PREFECT. Dear me, dear me! He excused himself for that servant business when I took the matter up with him.

LAUDISI. And that's information right from the source!

PREFECT. He says he does it to save money.

LAUDISI. He has to keep two establishments on one salary.

SIRELLI. Oh, we weren't criticising how he runs his

house; but I ask you as a matter of common sense: he is a man of some position, and do you think that this second wife of his, as he calls her, who ought to be a lady, would consent to do all the work about the house? . . .

AGAZZI. The hardest and most disagreeable work, you understand . . .

SIRELLI. . . . just out of consideration for the mother of her husband's first wife?

AGAZZI. Oh, I say, governor, be honest now! That doesn't seem probable, does it?

PREFECT. I confess it does seem queer . . .

LAUDISI. . . . in case this second woman is an ordinary woman!

PREFECT. Yes, but let's be frank. It doesn't seem reasonable. But yet, one might say—well, you could explain it as generosity on her part, and even better, as jealousy on his part. Lunatic or no lunatic, there is no denying that he's jealous!

(*A confused clamor of voices is heard from the next door*).

AGAZZI. My, I wonder what's going on in there!

(*Amalia enters from the door on the left in a state of great excitement*).

AMALIA. Signora Frola is here!

AGAZZI. Impossible! How in the world did she get in? Who sent for her?

AMALIA. Nobody! She came of her own accord!

PREFECT. Oh, no, please—just a moment! No! Send her away, madam, please!

AGAZZI. We've got to get rid of her. Don't let her in here! We must absolutely keep her out!

(*Signora Frola appears at the door on the left, trembling, besseching, weeping, a handkerchief in her hand. The people in the next room are crowding around behind her*).

SIGNORA FROLA. Oh, please, please! You tell them, Signor Agazzi! Don't let them send me away!

AGAZZI. But you must go away, madam! We simply can't allow you to be here now!

SIGNORA FROLA (*desperately*). Why? Why? (*Turning to Amalia*). I appeal to you, Signora Agazzi.

AMALIA. But don't you see? The prefect is there! They're having an important meeting.

SIGNORA FROLA. Oh, the prefect! Please, governor, please! I was intending to go and see you.

PREFECT. No, I am so sorry, madam. I can't see you just now! You must go away!

SIGNORA FROLA. Yes, I am going away. I am going to leave town this very day! I am going to leave town and never come back again!

AGAZZI. Oh, we didn't mean that, my dear Signora Frola. We meant that we couldn't see you here, just now, in this room. Do me a favor, please! You can see the governor by and by.

SIGNORA FROLA. But why? I don't understand! What's happened!

AGAZZI. Why, your son-in-law will soon be here! There, now do you see?

SIGNORA FROLA. Oh, he's coming here? Oh, yes, in that case . . . Yes, yes, . . . I'll go! But there was something I wanted to say to you people. You must stop all this. You must let us alone. You think you are helping me. You are trying to do me a favor; but really, what you're doing is working me a great wrong. I've got to leave town this very day because he must not be aroused. What do you want of him anyway? What are you trying to do to him? Why are you having him come here? Oh, Mr. Governor . . .

PREFECT. Come, Signora Frola, don't worry, don't

worry. I'll see you by and by and explain everything. You just step out now, won't you?

AMALIA. Please, Signora Frola . . . yes, that's right! Come with me!

SIGNORA FROLA. Oh, my dear Signora Agazzi, you are trying to rob me of the one comfort I had in life, the chance of seeing my daughter once in a while, at least from a distance! (*She begins to weep*) .

PREFECT. What in the world are you thinking of? We are not asking you to leave town. We just want you to leave this room, for the time being. There, now do you understand?

SIGNORA FROLA. But it's on his account, governor . . . it's on his account I was coming to ask you to help him! It was on his account, not on mine!

PREFECT. There, there, everything will be all right. We'll take care of him. And we'll have this whole business settled in a jiffy.

SIGNORA FROLA. But how . . . how can I be sure? I can see that everybody here hates him. They are trying to do something to him.

PREFECT. No, no, not at all! And even if they were, I would look after him. There, there, don't worry, don't worry!

SIGNORA FROLA. Oh, so you believe him? Oh, thank you; thank you, sir! That means that at least *you* understand!

PREFECT. Yes, yes, madam, I understand, I understand! And I cautioned all these people here. It's a misfortune that came to him long, long ago. He's all right now! He's all right now!

SIGNORA FROLA. . . . Only he must not go back to all those things.

PREFECT. You're right, you're quite right, Signora Frola, but as I told you, I understand!

SIGNORA FROLA. Yes, governor, that's it! If he compels us to live this way—well, what does it matter. That doesn't do anybody any harm so long as we're satisfied, and my daughter is happy this way. That's enough for me, and for her! But you'll look after us, governor. They mustn't spoil anything. Otherwise there's nothing left for me except to leave town and never see her again—never, not even from a distance. You must not irritate him. You must leave him alone. Oh, please!

(*At this moment a wave of surprise, anxiety, dismay, sweeps over the company. Everybody falls silent and turns to the door. Suppressed exclamations are audible.*)

VOICES. Oh! Oh! Look! There she is! Oh! Oh!

SIGNORA FROLA (*noticing the change in people, and groaning, all of a tremble*). What's the matter? What's the matter?

(*The company divides to either hand. A lady has appeared at the door in back. She is dressed in deep mourning and her face is concealed with a thick, black, impenetrable veil*).

SIGNORA FROLA (*uttering a piercing shriek of joy*). Oh, Lena! Lena! Lena! Lena!

(*She dashes forward and throws her arms about the veiled woman with the passionate hysteria of a mother who has not embraced her daughter for years and years. But at the same time from beyond the door in the rear another piercing cry comes. Ponza dashes into the room*).

PONZA. No! Julia! Julia! Julia!

(*At his voice Signora Ponza draws up stiffly in the arms of Signora Frola who is clasping her tightly. Ponza notices that his mother-in-law is thus desperately entwined about his wife and he shrieks desperately*).

PONZA. Cowards! Liars! I knew you would! I knew you would! It is just like the lot of you!

SIGNORA PONZA (*turning her veiled head with a certain austere solemnity toward her husband*). Never mind! Don't be afraid! Just take her away, just take her away! Please go away, now, both of you! Please go away!

(*Signora Frola, at these words, turns to her son-in-law and humbly, tremblingly, goes over and embraces him*).

SIGNORA FROLA. Yes, yes, you poor boy, come with me, come with me!

(*Their arms about each other's waists, and holding each other up affectionately, Ponza and his mother-in-law withdraw through the rear door. They are both weeping. Profound silence in the company. All those present stand there with their eyes fixed upon the departing couple. As Signora Frola and Ponza are lost from view, all eyes turn expectantly upon the veiled lady. Some of the women are weeping*).

SIGNORA PONZA. And what can you want of me now, after all this, ladies and gentlemen? In our lives, as you see, there is something which must remain concealed. Otherwise the remedy which our love for each other has found cannot avail.

PREFECT (*with tears in his eyes*). We surely are anxious to respect your sorrow, madam, but we must know, and we want you to tell . . .

SIGNORA PONZA. What? The truth? The truth is simply this. I am the daughter of Signora Frola, and I am the second wife of Signor Ponza. Yes, and—for myself, I am nobody, I am nobody . . .

PREFECT. Ah, but no, madam, for yourself . . . you must be . . . either the one or the other.

SIGNORA PONZA. Not at all, not at all, sir! No, for myself I am . . . whoever you choose to have me. (*Without removing her veil, she proudly casts a sweeping glance around at the company, and withdraws. They all stand looking after her. Profound silence on the stage).*

LAUDISI. Well, and there, my friends, you have the truth! But are you satisfied? Hah! hah! hah! hah! hah! hah! hah!

Curtain.

NOTE TO "RIGHT YOU ARE!"

A slight adaptation has been introduced into Signora Frola's explanation of her son-in-law's mania, Act I, p. 184, beginning "No, look, look, not that . . . etc." The Italian text reads:

SIGNORA FROLA. No guardino . . . guardino . . . Non è neanche lui! . . . Mi lascino dire. Lo hanno veduto— è così forte di complessione . . . violento . . . Sposando, fu preso da una vera frenesia d'amore . . . Rischiò di distruggere, quasi, la mia figliuola, ch'era delicatina . . . Per consiglio dei medici e di tutti i parenti anche dei suoi (che ora poverini non ci sono più)—gli si dovette sottrarre la moglie di nascosto, per chiuderla in una casa di salute . . . ecc."

A. L.

Printed in the United States
65939LVS00005B/262-276